What people

Spiritual Freedom in the Digital Age

Jason Gregory's latest book *Spiritual Freedom in the Digital Age* is a vibrant call to return to the essentials of life and to bring the value back into the art of *being*. Gregory, a lover of the human organism, tells us it is time to invest in ourselves. We are being desensitized by our addictions to an encroaching digital culture that can create anxiety and disconnection to the precious moments in life. This book reminds us to concentrate on cultivating focus and attention and to be truly present in our human relations. We must thank Gregory for this timely reminder to reevaluate our relationship to technology, and to understand the true value of human technology—the human being.

Kingsley L. Dennis, author of *The Sacred Revival: Magic, Mind & Meaning in a Technological Age*

Those interested in self-development and spiritual growth have a new set of hurdles to overcome. Hurdles previously unknown to the past masters; these are the hurdles of digital technology and the mind-numbingly addictive levels of distraction that they bring. I hope that people reading this book will actually take on board just how important the warnings and solutions given by Jason Gregory are if you really want the most out of life. What Jason has expertly written here is a book which echoes my own grave fears about the direction modern life is taking us.

Damo Mitchell, author of *A Comprehensive Guide to Daoist Nei Gong*

In *Spiritual Freedom in the Digital Age*, a writer who understands the true nature of the human mind and the way it manifests consciousness tells us how modern cyber-technology is rapidly degrading the quality of human consciousness and driving a huge wedge between human nature and Mother Nature. Jason Gregory, the author of several excellent books on spiritual awareness and the key role it plays in understanding reality and realizing our full potential in life, also has a working knowledge of the human brain and the way it assembles its view of the world on the inner screen of consciousness. In this book he explains how digital screens are replacing our inner screens as the primary source of consciousness in daily life, filling the mind with useless trivia scripted by media and distracting time and attention away from the important things in life, such as health and human relations. Many "tech-addicts" spend so much time plugged into the Internet that they now treat their own bodies like a piece of furniture or hardware—a chair to sit on, a garbage disposal for junk food, and a receptacle for vicarious pleasure on demand. So-called "social media" has become a hideaway for millions of asocial, and some very antisocial, people who have no social skills at all in real life, and yet this has become the norm today.

Gregory's book is a timely wake-up call for a world that is dozing off in The Big Sleep of cyber-space, a sleep so deep and far removed from human nature that it's turning much of the world into a beehive of automatons devoid of basic human values. But this is not a doomsday diatribe, like so many other books on the subject. It's a cogent appeal for caution and a "user's manual" with concrete suggestions for how people can use this technology in a way that does not disconnect their links with nature.

Daniel Reid, bestselling author of *The Tao of Health, Sex and Longevity* and *The Tao of Detox*

This book addresses a critically important issue: how to transform into the "new human" in what lies beyond the Information Age, using more than just our tech-addicted brain. To access our full potential, we must include heart, feelings, and body as equally enlightened parts of our total makeup. We are human for a reason! We don't transform by avoiding the physical world but by merging with it all the way. Pay attention to what Jason is saying here—it will wake you up!

Penney Peirce, author of *Transparency*, *Leap of Perception*, and *Frequency*

While commenting on the possible dangers of Artificial Intelligence, few pandits today are considering how our addiction to social media is transmuting our own intelligence into what is also literally artificial, that is "made by the human hand" rather than by nature. Jason Gregory shines a bright and thoughtful light on this blind spot in the present discourse, giving wise advice on how we might avoid becoming little more than windup toys made of meat.

Dana Sawyer, professor of religion and philosophy at the Maine College of Art, and the author of *Aldous Huxley: A Biography*

Also by this Author

Emotional Intuition for Peak Performance
ISBN 9781620559239

Effortless Living
ISBN 9781620557136

Fasting the Mind
ISBN 9781620556467

Enlightenment Now
ISBN 9781620555910

The Science and Practice of Humility
ISBN 9781620553633

Spiritual Freedom in the Digital Age

How to Remain Healthy and Sane in
a World Gone Mad

Spiritual Freedom in the Digital Age

How to Remain Healthy and Sane in a World Gone Mad

Jason Gregory

BOOKS

Winchester, UK
Washington, USA

JOHN HUNT PUBLISHING

First published by O-Books, 2022
O-Books is an imprint of John Hunt Publishing Ltd., 3 East St., Alresford,
Hampshire SO24 9EE, UK
office@jhpbooks.com
www.johnhuntpublishing.com
www.o-books.com

For distributor details and how to order please visit the 'Ordering' section on our website.

Text copyright: Jason Gregory 2021

ISBN: 978 1 78904 896 4
978 1 78904 897 1 (ebook)
Library of Congress Control Number: 2021932913

A CIP catalogue record for this book is available from the British Library.

Design: Stuart Davies

UK: Printed and bound by CPI Group (UK) Ltd, Croydon, CR0 4YY
Printed in North America by CPI GPS partners

We operate a distinctive and ethical publishing philosophy in
all areas of our business, from our global network of authors to
production and worldwide distribution.

Contents

Introduction – An Artificial Problem in a Natural World

If you're reading this book and the year is beyond 2050 then you are probably wondering, "Who the hell is this dinosaur that wrote this book? What a fossil!" Heck, you might be reading this in the present day and think exactly the same thing. But even though what you are about to read may seem archaic, it was not too long ago that what I will discuss in opposition to digital technology was the way life was. And, in actual fact, the way things were before digital technology is the way life always will be even if you don't believe it. We have just temporarily forgotten that way of life for now.

We've lost touch with the natural beauty in the world because we've bought into an artificial reality that could be taken away from us at any time. The simplicity of the natural world, which we are a part of, has been pushed into the background in favor of a shiny digital world. Our whole culture is being built around technological innovation, specifically digital technology.

If you are not technologically savvy you are considered an "old-timer" who is out of touch with modern culture. People assume that if you don't have a smartphone, tablet, desktop computer, laptop, and television, then you are disconnected and out of touch with the world. But what world are you *truly* out of touch with? (Bear with me, my answer to this question will unfold in the book.)

Just a very short time ago we had none of these digital devices and we were perfectly fine, and as my book contests we were in many cases better off without them. Don't get me wrong, I'm not totally against technological innovation (as I will discuss in Chapter 2) or the digital world. Social media, for example, has been extremely beneficial for my work and it has allowed myself to connect with my audience more intimately for which

I am grateful. But there is an ugly side to digital technology and social media that is not discussed in the mainstream. This book will explore the ugly side.

My main concern is how digital technology is influencing us and how it is affecting our sanity. You might have overlooked the impact of digital technology in your life, or you might be a millennial (often called Generation Y or Gen Y for people with birth years starting in the early 1980s to the mid-1990s as ending birth years) born in the early 1990s or part of iGeneration/iGen (often called Generation Z or Gen Z for young people born between 1995 and 2012) who grew up with access to the Internet joined at the hip, so you don't know any better.

We need to ask two serious questions about our digital device use: 1) Is it natural to be distracted all the time by digital devices? 2) Do we really need access to the Internet at our fingertips every moment of the day? Even though many of us don't want to admit it, we know the answer to both of these questions is *no*, but we just can't help ourselves. Sadly, millennials and iGen'ers believe being super connected and distracted are the way life is. Yet, no matter what age, when it comes to our smartphone we are like fidgety children with borderline ADHD. I am always astonished by everyone's fascination with digital technology, especially smartphones. Why is it so important to always play with your phone? I don't mean to be cynical, but are any of us truly that popular?

We currently live in a culture where we believe we should know "everything," or at least have access to the possibility of knowing everything. Our culture also ingrains in our mind that we should be "popular" and "relevant." This mix implies that we should be a popular version of Einstein, maybe close to Neil deGrasse Tyson, but even cooler, more popular, and smarter. Think of a hip version of Iron Man.

Our modern culture of popularity teaches us to stick out in front of the crowd for no apparent reason at all. We should be popular even though we don't know why. As a result, we are building a culture where we project an artificial persona into social media platforms as if this is a surefire way to popularity and being loved by the world. But this behavior exposes our psychological flaws and fears because our craving for attention is subtly an attempt to try and establish that we are worthy. We incorrectly believe we are worthless if we are not popular and respected by others. These sorts of deep-seated psychological issues that the digital world exposes are only the tip of the iceberg (I will go into these problems and many others throughout the book).

If we are fidgety with our phones and trying to be popular to feel worthy and accepted, then isn't this anxious use of digital devices questioning our sanity? What is wrong with just sitting still and breathing calmly while listening to the natural sounds of the world? Why don't we understand that *we are worthy no matter what* and that it is actually socialization that makes us feel worthless? Oh, that's right, we have built a culture that can't sit still for five seconds because we are trying to always distract our mind from the brutal reality we call our lives. We are addicted to busyness and so we identify with what we do rather than who we are.

Well, it's time to grow up and understand ourselves more intimately and reconnect with life itself. Until that time comes, we need to realize that we live in a culture not mature enough to use technology wisely for the benefit of humanity. Well, not yet anyway.

Are We Headed in the Right Direction? Or is the Digital World a Dead End?

Since we exhibit a level of immaturity with the use of digital technology, is it wise to go full steam ahead in that direction? If we keep falling down the rabbit hole of the digital world, who knows where we will end up and how a human being will be (if we will be human at all. More on this later in the book). If we keep pursuing this artificial life there is a trade-off. The trade-off is we will lose all contact and sensitivity to the natural world and also our own individual naturalness.

When was the last time you went into nature and just listened to her while observing your own natural breathing? Sounds like an odd question doesn't it. But that's what life itself *is* and we are trading it off for a world that is not real. A sad fact of reality is many people find the digital world much more interesting than the real world. But when we compare man-made technology to the natural world there is no comparison, because the mystery and complexity of nature is spellbinding.

You have direct access to the most sophisticated technology in the known universe, and I don't mean your smartphone. I'm talking about the human organism. *You* are the most sophisticated piece of technology in the known universe and most of us sadly don't know anything about it. But, on the other hand, we can teach someone to turn on the television and channel surf. Sadly, we hardly know anything about our body and mind. We're so caught up in the hustle and bustle of the world that we've forgotten we even have a body and mind. We forget about consciousness itself. We are like fish who aren't aware of the water.

We invest so much time and effort in everything else but ourselves. And I don't mean investing in your business, home, career, social media presence, and so on. I mean invest in your *actual* life, your health and sanity. How can we have a healthy and sane world if we don't invest in health and sanity on an individual level? It's not possible.

We strive for favorable circumstances externally, but often neglect our inner world. We don't consider how the digital world is affecting our mind. Having a sense of equanimity and harmony in our life is sadly not our concern in the digital age. We have built a world on comparison and competition, and those competitive juices are being directed into the digital world.

Our natural survival instincts are alerting us to keep up with everyone else by taking advantage of the digital revolution. We better invest our time and energy into our projected self-image of who we think we should be on our Instagram, Twitter, and Facebook accounts or people will know our lives are truly empty and boring (my sarcasm is noted). We spend so much time and energy trying to keep up with everyone else on social media that we totally forget about the *real* social aspect of life.

We lock our eyes onto our digital screens every waking moment. We clutch our smartphone to the very last minute as we lay down in bed and fire off that last tweet as if it couldn't wait until tomorrow. We'll wait for a bus and instead of making eye contact with someone else, we stare blankly into our glowing screens. Life is going by and you don't even know it. All you know is what the Facebook feed tells you to believe, as we vicariously live other people's digital lives.

These sorts of habits, such as scrolling the Twitter feed and seeing what is happening in people's lives on Facebook, are causing a lot of problems psychologically (I will discuss this at length throughout the book). This is where most of our time and energy is directed. But is it intelligent to invest all our time and energy into the digital world? Are we headed in the wrong direction? One thing is for sure, we are headed in an unnatural direction and it doesn't matter how lofty our goals are, because nature will always have the last word. So, I'm going to be unpopular and suggest we do a complete 180 degree turn and begin to head in the opposite direction.

Return to Your Nature

We have to reconsider where our time and energy are allocated if we are to complete this U-turn in thinking and way of life. We need to be honest with ourselves. Do you spend more time looking at a screen and anxiously anticipating screen time than you do anything else each day? We have to admit that, yes, we do spend most of our day staring into screens or anxiously anticipating screen time, and this wasted time compounds day after day, year after year.

We are not allocating our energy in the right places. Mindlessly living in the digital world has taken most of our time away, leaving no energy for nature or our own creativity and productivity. Maintaining our social media presence is the main energy drain. More time is spent on social media than our creativity, face-to-face communication, and time in nature. We have replaced the spontaneous beauty of life itself for digital upkeep. Our world is becoming less vibrant and alive as a result.

We have to continue traveling in the opposite direction if we wish to reclaim our mind and bring sanity back into the world. We have to drastically reduce our time spent in the digital world and reconnect with life as it truly *is*.

This book will explain how the digital world is destroying our mind and wasting our precious time. But, most importantly, it will explain a way out of this mess so you can reclaim who you truly *are*. Who you truly are brings value to the world. But, on the other hand, having a cool and spiffy social media presence is not intrinsically valuable. We're just trying to keep up with the Joneses.

Our intrinsic nature is what brings value to the world and that has nothing to do with being distracted by digital technology. What you have deep down within you is what benefits the world and your own life. It is the potential we all have, but sadly squander a lot of the time because of life's distractions (ahem, social media).

We have to stop being distracted to realize the magnitude of the problem. We have to reclaim our time from digital distractions and focus on resurrecting our innate naturalness. If we don't we run the risk of becoming robotic, meaning our thinking will become more mechanical than natural. This machinelike thinking has already begun in earnest, as our world is geared more towards analytical thinking which fuels rationality over and above everything else. This is a huge mistake. This machinelike thinking is against our spontaneous nature, which is what makes us human. Natural spontaneity is at the core of a human being. In Taoism they refer to this intrinsic naturalness in Chinese as *ziran*, which means *spontaneously of itself*. Nature and all of her children are spontaneously of itself. A machine, on the other hand, is not spontaneous or natural in any way. But, amazingly, we are starting to mimic a machine in our way of thinking and behavior (a super rationalist would obviously deny this since it exposes their unnatural behavior).

As a result, we are losing touch with natural spontaneity because socialization makes us compute and calculate everything as if nature is some sort of machine. Nature is not a machine and neither are we because, just in case you forgot, we are nature too. Yet we have constructed a society that is mechanically geared, where self-interest and digital devices destroy our naturalness. In turn, we destroy the environment to sustain our self-interested habits which include using digital technology to pacify our mind. Isn't it ironic that the more unnatural we become the less we care about the environment? We are intrinsically linked to nature and once one aspect of nature is acting cancerously it affects the whole ever so slowly. We have sold the spontaneous experience of life in favor of a life where we think we have control of our destiny. For those of you who have lived a while, you would know that the spontaneity of life has a way of throwing your best-laid plans out the window. As a result, you have to learn to adapt and grow from unexpected circumstances.

But in the digital age we don't believe we have to adapt to life because we have access to all information at our fingertips which seemingly allows us to navigate the obstacles of life. And you might be able to navigate through some obstacles, but life will continue to happen beyond your control or perception of how life should be. You can't just "crop and delete" life's spontaneous experience.

Since our world has become more rational, we think that we can analyze life to its nth degree and so we can control it for our benefit. But in reality, this will never be true. And yet, this is why the digital world is so appealing, because we can control our experience in that world. We can control the information we want to absorb, where we want to travel (web surf). We can even avoid trolls with the click of a block button. Seems like a utopia, but it's not.

The digital world is also appealing because we can momentarily escape life's brutality. And yes, life can be brutal sometimes, but by diving into your phone those things you have to face won't magically disappear. The digital world acts the same as any addiction: when life is tough, we lean on a substance to try and escape life or escape, most commonly, ourselves. As with any addiction, we begin to become dissociated with ourselves and the world around us. So, the addiction we have to our phones and other digital devices is the beginning of our dissociation with our own naturalness and the environment. Hence, we only care about the next time we can mindlessly be in the digital world. Everything else is just a waiting period to be there. As a result, an addict loses their naturalness because all of their energy is spent in unconsciously suppressing their nature.

Fidgeting with our smartphones, or any other digital device, only enhances our unnaturalness which leads to chronic stress and anxiety. Digital devices ramp up our stress and anxiety, and most of us don't even know we live in this unnatural state of mind most of the day. Sadly, most of us don't know what an equanimous mind feels like. The digital world only aggravates stress and anxiety which ultimately destroy our nature if we live in that state of mind more often than not. Digital technology can only enhance unnaturalness in us because it is not natural. It is not natural to us.

Digital technology is not like using the physical design of a violin to train our body to the point that the beauty of Bach can emanate from the instrument. But instead, the digital world has nothing to do with the nature of your body because it is a world that keeps you locked in the mind. As a result, we disconnect from our body and reside in our own private sanctuary in our mind.

This disembodied state leads not only to an unhealthy and insane individual, but also an unhealthy and insane world. Our naturalness depends on mind-body holism (I will explain this at length in Chapter 5). Our mind and body are embodied, not separate. The digital world is trying to pull us out of our bodies (nature), where we just dwell in the illusion of our mind. We need to return to our nature before it's too late. If we don't take seriously what this book explains, then we can't complain about the insane world that awaits us.

This is the Most Important Book of Our Time

This book offers a chance for us to reassess the direction we are heading. This book provides an opportunity to stop and pause your life so that you can reconsider what is important to a human life. Most importantly, it will show us a way of reclaiming the innate naturalness that we're slowly losing. We need to reclaim our naturalness if we are to live in a healthy and sane world. But this requires all of us to reevaluate our relationship with the digital world.

For those reading this book who are always joined at the hip to a smartphone, it will require hard work to break that unnatural habit you have developed. Instead of being addicted to distracting the mind, we need to settle the mind. Only then can we give our best to reach our full potential.

A mind full of noise can do nothing but seek more noise in an endless cycle of entertainment seeking. If we don't reassess the direction we are headed then we face a future as an organism out of sync with the natural world (if that has not already begun). Our attraction to the digital world is like sending our divorce papers to the natural world. We are separating ourselves from the natural world, that which we are and that which we came from. At the moment it's a trial separation. But this divorce will end tragically if we continue down this path. I don't mean only an ecological crisis, but I also mean in the health and sanity of the human race. If we are unhealthy and insane, we will continue to drive ecological destruction and the premature end of our species. I know I may sound all "doom and gloom," but this is a very real reality if we don't reclaim our mind and innate naturalness.

This book will expose how the digital world is destroying our mind and naturalness. But it will also show you a way to reconnect with the spontaneous reality of life without feeling anxious about it. This book will explain how simple life used to be and how in simplicity there was an innocence we've lost from being overly busy and trying to know everything. As a result, we've lost touch with the heart and live in a rational world where getting things done and being "successful" are at the top of the totem pole. This book will expose this common attitude for being unnatural and part of a psychological condition that is out of touch with the natural world. Don't get me wrong, being productive and successful are not inherently negative, but when our sole focus is on them, we lose a little piece of our naturalness piece by piece. We lose our innocence and become too ambitious, too headstrong. These unnatural tendencies are being channeled into the digital world.

We believe the digital playground of social media is important to our success. But nothing could be further from the truth. What is truly important is your productivity and creativity. Sure, social media can accentuate both and is a good resource for promotion, but social media use for the sake of itself is kryptonite for both. It's an unnatural distraction. If you want to be truly creative and productive you need large quantities of undistracted time to go deep in your work. No other creator in the world has created lasting work any other way. To achieve meaningful work, we need to be skillful at a craft which again requires large quantities of time over years and decades to master. And our skill is evoked from our mind-body integrated system. Skill is our innate naturalness in action, expressing the spontaneous beauty of life.

The more we head in the direction of the digital world, the less creative and skillful our world becomes (I am mindful that there are a lot of skillful filmmakers using software to create content for platforms such as YouTube, myself included. Though, this is an anomaly. Keep in mind that YouTube is only used to upload the work and if you spend too much time on it or any other social media you still won't be as creative or productive as you could and should be). It's hard to master any craft if you're checking your social media feeds every day, every hour, or in some sad cases, *all the time*. We've lost our precious time to reach our full potential. We sold that possibility so we can be entertained and relevant. This book will give you the tools to reclaim your time so the world can see who you truly are and the great gifts you have to offer.

We all have so much to offer and we all have an infinite storehouse of potential within us. But we have to put the effort in to refrain from distraction in this world, i.e. the digital world. A human being is human when we express that infinite potential dwelling in our naturalness. We just have to give ourselves time, undistracted time, to realize this. We have to aspire to be human again. And a human is not a rational computer that mimics the function of a digital device. But instead, a human being is an integral part of nature as nature, designed to express the most beautiful and subtle qualities of the universe.

We can all express our nature if we are willing to push back on digital devices distracting us. If we don't, the ultimate trade-off is we will lose our naturalness in favor of a mechanical world that believes any error or failure is an enemy. A human being is not designed to be a practical machine, but rather we are life and life includes everything. So, this means we have no "crop and delete" option but rather we are designed for an unbridled experience of life. The digital world is inculcating a negative perspective in our minds that life should bend to our will because this is how it is in the digital world. This is a common trait of entitled people which is sadly infecting ordinary people due to the digital world. But life will always have its way and we can either act like selfish entitled people or we can grow up and understand life better.

This book is the most important book of this era because it gives us a last chance to reassess the direction we are heading both collectively and individually. Our choices right now are what will determine our future. A human life is precious and its naturalness should be preserved and not destroyed. This book is not concerned about what is best for the tech industry or the economy, but rather it's concerned with the beautiful intrinsic nature of a human that we are sadly losing.

Silicon Valley's Most Feared Book

This book is everything the tech industry fears. Silicon Valley built its name on people willfully participating in the digital experience. The foundation of the digital world was built in Silicon Valley, and it is continuing to push new boundaries. Silicon Valley, and the entire tech industry, depends on your engagement and your interest in digital technology. What would happen if people began to use their time wisely and were not overly interested in the digital world? Don't get me wrong, I don't want anyone in the tech industry to be out of business and I believe being connected with people on social media from all parts of the world can be a positive thing if we use it intelligently, but first and foremost my main concern is the human condition regardless of what is good for business.

Actually, no one in business overly cares about the human condition because, whether anyone in the tech industry wants to admit it or not, the financial bottom line and social influence are what matters most. No one is considering the human condition, not even consumers. Everyone is on the digital bandwagon without considering if this is leading to health and sanity or deterioration and insanity. Nobody is in the business of telling people to refrain from overusing digital technology. And yet, here I am, such an unpopular choice but an honest and necessary one.

In the end, it shouldn't be up to me to expose the effects digital technology is having on the human condition. The tech industry is either turning a blind eye to the negative impacts on humanity or they are so blinded by their progress that they themselves are out of touch with reality. Surely, they must know that the digital world fuels mental health issues such as chronic stress, anxiety, depression, and in some extreme cases suicide. Not to mention the unhealthy lives we live from staring at screens every day.

Has anyone in the tech industry considered these negative impacts on human life? Is it their responsibility to do so? Some of you may suggest it is not their responsibility because it is just the nature of capitalism. The negative health impacts are too diverse to slap a warning label on digital technology like we do with a packet of cigarettes. So, we can't rely on the tech industry to be concerned about the human condition. This means it is up to you to take your power back and rediscover your naturalness. We can't do that if we are not willing to refrain from the digital world. You need to own that responsibility to reap the benefits. Taking your power back means a return to the simple life, which is natural. When we simplify our life, we begin to regain our intrinsic health and sanity because they are natural to us. It's a choice of simplicity over speed. The digital world speeds up our life, depleting our nervous system leading to stress, anxiety, depression, and other mental health issues (I will discuss this at length in Part III). Simplicity, on the other hand, nourishes our nervous system leading to creativity, equanimity, and peace.

Simplicity is definitely not Silicon Valley's concern, but it should be yours. It is only in simplifying your life that you will understand your naturalness as an integral part of the entire ecosystem. That simplicity and naturalness can never be destroyed, but they can be forgotten in the humdrum of life. We can lose sense of their innate importance to us when we have invested all of our time and energy in an illusory world that could disappear at any time. This book is about giving you the opportunity to understand the human condition and how important it is to never lose sense of your simple nature, which is the key to the health and sanity of our world. We need to reconnect with an older and simpler way of living so that we can use technology wisely. We must disconnect from technology to reconnect with nature which is who we truly are.

Part I

The Positive and Negative Impact of Technology

Chapter 1

The Evolution of Digital Culture and Robotic Behavior

My dad always told me how life used to be better. He would tell me how Coca-Cola used to taste better, how KFC was once clean and digestible, and how people used to say hello to strangers and look people in the eye. I just thought that was my dad being Dad. I thought he was jaded and didn't like the world because he had a tough upbringing (a whole other conversation). I mean, I was only six years old and he was telling me how JFK, Martin Luther King Jr., and Malcolm X were all assassinated by the CIA and how the world is run by rich bankers (I'm not implying any of this is true, but it is what my dad believed and told me).

When he was telling me at six that I should know this sort of information, I just thought he was a crackpot because I had better things to do, such as play on my Sega Master System. So, when he used to tell me that life used to be better, I was like, "Yeah right!" But I was only a snotty-nosed little kid, what did I really know? My perception of that old crackpot has changed over the years. Considering the depth of my work, I've met some wise people in my life, but I still regard my dad as one of the smartest people I've known. He was completely misunderstood and he had his own flaws, but who doesn't.

I didn't know it at six years old, but those life lessons he gave me would still stick with me until today and be even more important now than ever. To my own astonishment, I've begun to start sounding like my dad. I'm explaining to millennials and iGen'ers how good life used to be, how pure and innocent the old days were.

I spent hardly any time indoors in my youth. Computer games were only just coming out, and even though my brother and I had a Sega, I still spent most of my time with my friends outdoors mucking around and causing trouble (in the best possible way of course). We would spend all day riding our bikes, kicking the football at the park, swimming in the local creek where we would jump off the railway bridge into the water and also coat ourselves in mud playing a game we called "army" in the mangroves as if we were big Arnie (Arnold Schwarzenegger) in the film *Predator*.

There was just so much fun to have and so little time to experience it. In my home town of Mackay there was no McDonald's up until I was nine (1990), so we ate local burgers and they tasted like real food as opposed to plastic. The dress sense was funky, the haircuts more outlandish (I had a prickle cut), and you could distinguish a musician's music from another's music. It was such a cool time to be alive. The 80s and 90s had a certain vibe about them. They are very vivid in everyone's memory. Why?

Echoes of a Vibrant Culture

Vanilla Ice, a famous rapper and one of the paragons of a hip culture pre-digital era, sympathizes with my dad as he believed that the 90s was the last great decade because there was a certain culture and feel to the 90s which we haven't had since the year 2000. It's hard to argue with his viewpoint. There was a certain dress sense and music that defined the 90s and we often find ourselves marveling at that time (or before then) either by listening to the music of the 90s or by reviving its dress sense. But, as Vanilla Ice explained in an interview with Patrick Bet-David on the Valuetainment Podcast,[1] since the year 2000 until present day nothing has really defined these decades other than computers. The sense of a culture has been lost (well, that is in the Western world). Just compare the 2000s to the 90s and 80s, the 2000s have no distinct flavor and dare I say it, are dull.

Millennials and iGen'ers would surely disagree, but they too find themselves looking back in time with a sense of awe. Even our dress sense since the 90s hasn't evolved much. But when we look at the 50s, 60s, 70s, 80s, and 90s, there is a certain culture to all of them that is distinguishable. You can just see the way someone is dressed and you know the decade. We can just look at the evolution of Elton John's dress sense to know the decade. But this is not noticeable since the turn of the millennium. And yet, will millennials and iGen'ers be saying the same things to the youth when they are my age? Or are my dad, Vanilla Ice, and myself just the crackpots I sensed in my youth? Well, maybe Vanilla Ice and myself are considering my dad told me everything he did in the 80s. But if he thought it was bad then, if he was still alive, he would surely scoff at the way life is now.

This is not a feeling isolated to my dad, Vanilla Ice, and myself. It is something many of us feel, but we can't quite put our finger on it. Is this some sort of cycle where we get older and reflect on how good things once were? Do we just miss our youth? Do we become more jaded and discontent with the present world as we get older? Is this some sort of psychological defect or was my dad truly onto something that we are missing today?

An Empty Culture Lacking Substance

Since the year 2000 the Western world has lost a sense of a unique and funky culture. But this is not just isolated to the West. You find now in places such as India, China, Nepal, the Middle East, and Thailand a sense that their culture is slowly fading, especially among affluent people of those regions. For example, you could go from a small town in the south of India called Tiruvannamalai steeped in Hindu culture and then go to Mumbai and you'll think you're on another planet. Mumbai has turned into a modern metropolis hellbent on selling their Hindu culture for a tasteless materialist culture devoid of life, all in the name of "progress."

Mumbai might be unique in India, but this tasteless culture is developing in many large cities around the world. When you're in Mumbai you somewhat feel the same as you do in other large cities around the world. I'm writing these words in Brisbane and that sense of something missing is here in the same way it is in New York, London, Paris, Seoul, and Tokyo, just to name a few.

There is a *sameness* developing in the world which is very dull. It has no life in it. Instead, it is functionable and very mechanical. This is modern culture, the culture that is being spread across the world at the expense of rich traditional cultures. And we should not be mistaken, modern culture is missing actual *culture*. Modern culture is actually devoid of anything we would consider culture.

Modern "culture" is basically a mechanically functioning society driven by a practical philosophy of life, cloaked in the illusion of progress. Practicality has taken over beauty, leaving us with a dull world where everything is increasingly the same. As a result, modern culture has no edge, no groove. It is devoid of error and our mentality is reflecting it. In a mechanical world we begin to act like lifeless robots where we have to overly mind our Ps and Qs.

Political Correctness is Unnatural

We are developing an over-the-top political correctness in the world which we all know deep down is not natural. It has a certain stench about it. The stench of political correctness infects our mind, producing individuals who have disconnected from their intrinsic nature and beauty. These individuals we all know too well. They are the over-the-top social justice warriors and righteous people in general, who brandish their own personal agendas on the world. They will lynch anybody's character for the slightest error in their eyes with zero forgiveness. This ignorant PC attitude has given rise to cancel culture online, which is undoubtably the dumbest way to behave. How you can apparently cancel someone is absurd and also impossible (unless these immature people actually want people to die). That our hate is so fervent that we would want to cancel someone (whatever that means) is an example of what a world would look like with no forgiveness or empathy (not to mention intelligence) for our brothers and sisters of the world. A stinky culture plagued by political correctness is under the misguided belief that there is a specific way that everybody should live their life and an artificial language (political correctness) of maintaining this way of life.

This is the attitude of the Alt-Left extreme liberals and their woke ideology is considered the "right" way of life. This has gotten to the point that it has become a religion and if you're not on board then you're in their crosshairs. If we are not politically correct then "they" will savage you. To counter such a savage attack, it is in our best interest to be vegan, use gender neutral pronouns, believe in equality of outcome, ride a bicycle or drive a Tesla, and learn to hunt in packs as they do (again, my sarcasm is noted). I'm not saying that any of those views are wrong because they are all subjective opinions and viewpoints. But what is wrong is to impose your own personal beliefs and agendas on anyone else as if your view of the world is the truth. Our bible-thumping habits obviously die hard. If we don't fall in line with this politically correct attitude then we will be condemned, humiliated, and ostracized. This is the world a tasteless culture produces. This is a politically correct hell. And hell is when we divorce from our intrinsic nature and instead employ a robotic behavior.

But this doesn't mean the political right are right. Both political ideologies have their own flaws and extreme attitudes. Both are built on their own subjective beliefs and opinions which is the actual heart of the problem (a whole other conversation about the illusion of identity which has no place in this book).

There is no one person with a universal temperament of being either liberal or conservative. We are truly a mix of both, and until we reach that level of maturity, we cannot have the adult conversation we need to have to understand each other deeply. Personally, politics gives me a headache and I'm astonished at how many people are interested in it. There is a lot more to life than to listen to a bunch of people wield their subjective opinions. I am neither left nor right. Call me ambidextrous, or better yet, call me human.

Trying to be politically correct all the time is robotic, leading to a very mechanically geared analytical state of mind. This creates lifeless people who are more concerned about making a mistake than actually living naturally. This robotic politically correct mentality is hindering real social progress because we are developing a terrible tendency of individually policing one another with a woke version of censorship. This misinformed attitude blocks the free flow of ideas that invariably help us evolve as a species.

My wife has been affected by this in the workplace. She feels alone in her work at times because what she is interested in conflicts with her employees. For example, she once thought about discussing the negative impact of social media with her colleagues, but she knew she would be shut down and ostracized because her colleagues defend their smartphones as if they are their children. It is an evolutionary strategy to stay quiet on certain sensitive topics so that one doesn't incur any harm. I sympathize with my wife because I too have engaged in such discussions only to be laughed out of the room by a bunch of people hypnotized by their phones.

As I mentioned, the big problem is that when many of us, especially those of you who are intelligent, remain silent because the politically correct crowd are monitoring your thoughts with their own ideology, then this will handicap true social progress until this whole childish game is over. We essentially become a prisoner to other so-called "progressive" crowds' misguided beliefs. This is a form of censorship we are individually imposing on other people, which wouldn't look out of place in Communist China.

An extreme example of this is how the woke liberal leftist media negatively portrays Hindus in India, keep in mind the majority of people in India are Hindu. Hinduphobia is not new. Throughout history Hindus have had to deal with invasion after invasion, but they have always persisted and actually absorbed other cultures into the fabric of Indian culture, and this is a credit to their inclusive Hindu spiritual beliefs. But this inclusive Hindu nature is not highlighted by foreign news media. Usually the Western temperament is to sympathize with those who have been on the wrong end of injustice, but that is not the case for Hindus. Leftist media, especially, condemn Hindus and judge them according to their own beliefs which are foreign to Hindu thought. This leftist attitude is classically known as "intellectual imperialism." As if it wasn't enough that Hindus had to deal with physical imperialism, now they have to deal with the intellectual imperialists. When does it end?

It is a real dangerous game when one culture judges another based on their own beliefs and agenda. The danger is evident and obvious in the intellectual imperialism waged against Hindus. I won't get into the fine details of the left's problem with Hinduism, or why the left believe Hindus are right-wingers, which is really stupid and a view based on Western political ideologies. But the crux of the problem is that Hindus in India are finally standing up for their identity and place in the world. This attitude conflicts with the leftist media because Hindu beliefs, politics, and customs are a lot different to what is deemed politically correct/moral in the West. Ashish Dhar, the co-founder of Pragyata and Upword Foundation and the Director of Operations at The Indic Collective Trust, explains in his work that it is hard to have an opinion on the Hindu tradition and the general diversity of Indian civilization if you have no real "skin in the game."

Foreign media have no real skin in the game in regards to the plight of Hindus over the centuries, which sadly has resulted in some Hindus feeling ashamed of their tradition. Imagine the uproar if Hindus were vocal and had opinions about the political situation in the US? But people in general in India wouldn't do that because they have no real skin in the game and they are more worried about their day-to-day life. If we have no skin in the game then we should mind our own business. But this conflicts with politically correct ideologies because they are built on being a stickybeak [busybody]. Being a stickybeak only leads to conflict. But this politically correct mentality is being embraced around the world and is enhanced through social media.

Actually, social media trains people subtly to police other people, even strangers. This has happened through the invention of the comment section on social media platforms. What seemed like an innocent application has turned into a tool where random people can police your thoughts. We experience this mainly through strangers, people we've never met, which is not natural. Being exposed to a stranger's opinion of your thoughts, beliefs, etc., is the same as foreign media having an ill-informed opinion on the Hindu way of life. So, before you troll someone online or police a person you don't know, think about how those actions will subtly reinforce an unnatural politically correct attitude and mentality within your mind. Social media is contributing to that (more on social media later in later chapters).

Ask yourself this, would you pull up a stranger in the street and tell them they are wrong and their beliefs stupid? Of course, all healthy and sane people would not do that because that is not how society works. Being nice and having common courtesy for others is a crucial part of our success as a species.

The way we behave offline should be how we behave online. If you alter your behavior online then you are likely developing a subtle psychopathy and are not a consistent individual. We already have police, so we don't need to police each other, especially our thoughts. It is unnatural for us to speak to people offline negatively so we need to behave like that online. Being politically correct is a subtle form of intellectual imperialism we impose on each other and we didn't evolve to monitor each other's thoughts based on our own subjective worldview.

Political correctness is completely unnatural. Political correctness is under the guise that perfection is attainable (or what they assume is perfection). This is bullshit! Perfection is a mirage. We all fuck-up every now and then, it's cool, no big deal, it's what makes us human and keeps us grounded. Fucking up is how we learn and grow; it couldn't be otherwise.

We are not computers. We can't just crop and delete life to suit our idealistic goals or those of others who try and hold us hostage to their beliefs. Life runs counter to your idealistic politically correct goals. We will never eradicate mistakes and failures from our life, even though social justice warriors and righteous people are anxiously trying.

We grow and transform from failures; this is how the natural world evolves. No matter how lofty your aims are, we can't uproot that natural growth constitution. Politically correct people fear this because it completely disarms their ideology and reveals to them that they are not ultimately in control of their lives. They themselves are the ones in conflict with the world because they have bought into the idea of right and wrong, which are human ideals that have nothing to do with nature. Don't get me wrong, there is a code of ethics that binds society, but there is no absolute "right" that all should adjust to. Even if there was, which culture is it part of? Which culture is right? Which political ideology is right?

This is where social justice warriors and righteous people

look stupid because they base their idealism on a Western liberal view and so they don't even consider traditional cultures in other countries. This is hypocrisy. This is the same as self-interested tyrannical governments going around bombing small nations under the guise of peace. They both have the same attitude; they are both fearful that there are people and other nations who have a different psychology and beliefs. Their way of dealing with this is by brute force, condemnation, humiliation, and ostracization. Both the righteousness of social justice warriors and self-interested tyrannical governments are unnatural, and sadly produce a stale world full of political correctness.

We lose our humanity when we act in this manner. Life isn't mechanical or biased to our view; instead it is natural and when we don't realize this then we begin to stink. In Zen Buddhism this is called "to stink of Zen." This means we have a stench about us when we are too pious, basically too gooey and cringeworthy. In Zen they believe that having this politically correct attitude just reveals that you are truly at odds with your own humanity.

We stagnate like motionless water when there is no life moving through it. Naturally we should accept our own humanity and what it means to sustain a human life. But we are out of sync with our own humanity when we think mechanically about life.

Political correctness and an analytical culture are not natural to anyone, they are the result of specific training of one function of the mind that we are completely unaware of. This specific training happens the day we walk into school. Now this is not a beat up on education, but instead it is about the pitfalls of only focusing on education minus playfulness that extends into our adult life.

All Work and No Play is Killing Us

Education and the majority of the working environment are focused on the analytical perspective, intellectual training.

This training drags us continually into one region and function of the brain, namely the prefrontal cortex (PFC) and the cold cognition. The cold cognition is the function of the PFC. The cold cognition is the cognitive control centers in the brain, residing in the PFC. The cold system is self-conscious, slow, deliberate, effortful, and it is the part of our mind we refer to as ourselves, the "I." It is associated with the subjective experience of agency, choice, and concentration. Our educational and vocational training overcompensates for the cold cognition, leading to super analytical and rational people devoid of naturalness.

The *natural* function of cognition is what is suppressed when we primarily train the cold cognition. This natural function is called the hot cognition. The hot system is the cognitive function that is automatic, spontaneous, effortless, mostly unconscious, and what is the primary driver of emotions. It operates automatically and is fast and spontaneous, with little or no effort. In the hot cognitive process, there is no sense of voluntary control (I will discuss this more in length in Chapter 5). As a result, the hot cognition is the foundational function of the mind that evokes our naturalness and natural response to life. Plus, it is also the function we access when we are having fun. It is that part of our mind that enjoys play, and this is essential because the mind is nourished by play. Children know this up until a certain age when intellectual training takes over. Unfortunately, play becomes background noise due to all of our education. And when we become adults, in general, we are way too serious and a super bore to those of us who have kept a sense of our innocence and ability to have fun.

In the Eastern spiritual traditions, they explain how it is imperative to return to our childlike mind because seriousness is killing us slowly both individually and collectively. This childlike mind is how we can have fun and playfully engage with life without being too serious about it. Fun and playfulness, within the hot cognition, are how we express our spontaneous nature as nature does.

Our seriousness destroys nature, because if we are analytical about everything then we will begin to act mechanically. Our emphasis on political correctness is a gross aspect of the mind that only accesses the cold cognition. We are stinking of Zen more and more each generation. So, we need to be mindful about how we teach our children. We are so focused on cognitive intelligence that we forget all about the foundation of emotional and moral intelligence. This attitude is rife in most parts of the world and it is how we are choosing to train our youth. I've witnessed this firsthand all over the world. Especially when I taught English to Chinese and Korean children.

In China and South Korea school students undergo inhumane rote learning where there is not a second spared in the day for play and just letting a kid be a kid. Every minute is devoted to learning, with no time for play. This unnatural training leads to all sorts of psychological problems that children should not have to deal with at such a young age. The effects are disastrous. In South Korea, for example, there are many children who have jumped out of apartment building windows because there is just too much pressure on their young mind. As a result, South Korea has one of the highest rates of teen suicides. It's just not natural or healthy to overcompensate for the cold cognitive functions.

Our nature resides in the hot cognition and if we continue to suppress our nature then we are left with a world that just discerns between what is subjectively right and wrong according to a morality that is not natural, but instead stinky. Analytical thinking, where we cut the world up into "this" and "that" with our intellect, leads to an unnatural state of mind where we lose our sense of fun because we begin to mimic machines inside our head. We begin to act like automatons with no spontaneous joy. Resulting from our machinelike analytical thinking, we incorrectly assume we are in control of our life and our destiny.

This attitude is what drives our modern culture, if we have the audacity to call it a culture.

The Digital World is Modern Culture

Our overuse of analytical thinking (cold cognition) matches the process and functioning of the digital world. Everything is technical and can be controlled to a certain degree. This suits modern people, especially for millennials and iGen'ers who unfortunately don't know any different. But this is not just the case for millennials and iGen'ers, as we see an increasing number of older people sucked into the digital world. Our overtraining of cold cognition does not suit the real world because it is out of sync with it. A mind like a calculator will seek an environment that suits it, and that's the digital world.

People have always struggled and suffered from *real life* because they don't understand it nor themselves. Only when we abide in our innate nature will we know ourselves and life, without the need for intellectual discernment. Nature is not some rational thing that we can bend with our logic. Instead, nature is completely irrational because nature is spontaneously of itself. Life itself is spontaneous. It is constantly happening to you, but we want to believe we are happening to it. Life is irrational because it is beyond logic and we too are primarily irrational even though we believe we are mainly rational.

We belong to this irrational life. We are spontaneously of itself because we are nature. The real world is our home and we are part of it as it. But our focus on only training the cold cognition has led us to believe that we are separate from nature and in some sense opposed by it. We think in this way because we can't control nature. Nature is happening beyond our logical view.

An analytical mind is anxious when it can't control its reality. This disembodied rationality leads to an idiotic conflict with the real world. This conflict comes down to our real lack of control. And because we lack control in real life, the digital world becomes more appealing. It gives us a sense of control (well, until your hard drive crashes or a troll annoys you). We can control our digital experience, where we go, what we watch and read, who we communicate with, and so on.

This sense of control is appealing, sucking people in more and more. For example, when smartphones first came on the market, they were not too much of a distraction at the beginning. They were originally designed so we didn't have to carry both our iPod and cell phone, as Steve Jobs explained when he introduced the iPhone to the world in his famous 2007 Macworld keynote. But as we grew accustomed to using one and its applications began to be more user friendly, we started to increase our usage. It's at such a drastic stage now that it is quite plausible to suggest on average a person spends more time looking at screens during the day than just our natural experience away from screens.

Our days are organized around the time we can spend in the digital world. Everything else we do in our day is a way station before we can play with our digital devices. Every break at work is spent on our phones and sometimes for those working in offices we might sneak some social media time in while the boss isn't watching. We finish school or work and rush home to log in to the digital world and switch off the real world. Instead of playing and enjoying yourself in the real world, your relaxation time is spent in the digital world.

For example, we don't want to play with a ball in the park any more, not even kids, because we can play fake ball games in a fake world and troll people we don't know in that fake (digital) world all from the comfort of our home. What a dream life (I know, sarcasm again). Our hidden and isolated sense of play/fun in the digital world is free from the repercussions of our actions. We can allow our demons and bad habits to run amok and nobody is the wiser. This shelter we feel in the digital world frees us from the accountability we need to exercise in real life. The digital world allows us to live in our own private lives separate from the whole world. This behavior develops a lot of problems in the psyche (I will explain this more in Chapter 5).

We are out of sync with the real world. Real life is on pause and who knows when we'll press the play button. We are so intoxicated with the digital world that we are unknowingly destroying our innocent nature.

Losing Our Innocence

With access to all information at our fingertips we could be excused for thinking that this is a positive thing. We've always wanted access to more information, we want to know more. But at what expense are we willing to know everything? Are you willing to trade-off parts of your innate nature just so you can know more? Why I ask these questions is because we lose something precious to our nature when we begin to know too much: our innocence.

Most people don't know this because they don't pause and reflect, as we are in environments where everyone else is trying to know as much or more than anyone else. When you're in a culture geared in this way, it is hard to know that innocence is disappearing. But if you've traveled the world experiencing other cultures then it is so obvious that the world is losing its innocence at the hands of knowing too much.

I've traveled the world extensively and have spent almost a decade in Asia. I spend a lot of time in rural India and Nepal, sometimes living there for six months in each place. When I'm there, there is an overwhelming sense of innocence in the people, even though in most cases they are less fortunate materialistically than people in the West. They look you in the eye, greet you as if you were God, listen deeply to every word, and have a smile as innocent and pure as a child. When you are around people like this you naturally feel more peaceful and they bring you back to your own innocence which has been covered over with knowing too much.

Learned people often go into these areas and start telling the people how to think and act, as if learned people know best. The irony is that it is the learned person who needs to learn about intrinsic human nature from just being in the presence of those innocent people. But what happens is the learned person comes off as an asshole because, just like many Western intellectuals, they decide what is best for everyone. We become this type of asshole when we learn too much. As a result, we lose our innocence, not to mention our humility.

The digital world is fueling this fire because having access to all information is a relatively new phenomenon, and so we are intrigued. We become addicted to learning and devalue *being*. There is nothing wrong with learning per se, but learning *too much* about everything destroys our purity. Actually, trying to learn too much scatters our mind, which coincidently means we don't absorb deeply all the information we are trying to learn if there is an overload.

Our mind is analog, not digital. You just can't upload information to your mind and think you understand what it is you're trying to know. It takes time to zero in on a subject matter to know it completely. But the digital world is developing a culture where skimming over the surface of a subject matter is normal for one to say they know it. We don't learn something completely, but instead we learn in soundbites. Craftsmen, for example, dedicate their life to their craft and learn what is necessary for their craftmanship to grow, keeping their innocence intact during the process. There is always more to learn about their craft which inculcates humility. Their humble attitude of not knowing keeps them innocent. On the other hand, in a soundbite culture we think we know everything so our innocence disappears.

There is a growing trend of teenagers these days who believe they know everything. This sort of know-it-all attitude comes from a life lived in the digital world. As teenagers we think we know everything, but the digital world actually fools them into really believing it. They don't know life has many wonderful experiences in store for them. Because they "know" everything from overlearning, they lose their sense of wonder and don't see the value of life. As a result, many teenagers are depressed because they believe they have come to the end of knowledge. This is disastrous and not natural.

The digital world might be able to explain a lot of information, but it can never give you the natural experience of life, where the majority of the real lessons are learned. That can only happen when we make a conscious decision to refrain from the digital world and return to simplicity. We have to be fine with not knowing. In reality, we can never know everything. Innocence is not lost because we know everything, but because we *believe* we know everything. The digital world fuels this delusion.

When we choose to simplify our life, we regain our innocence and enjoy the sweet nectar of life itself. This is more important than knowing everything. We don't have this innocence anymore because we lost our simplicity. Why my dad always believed life was better in the past is because as the years go on, we lose simplicity. Life was better because the simple life we know is slowly disappearing, and with it our innocence. This process has sped up since the year 2000 because computers and the Internet started to complicate our lives even more.

With the speed and complex nature of the digital world our intrinsic simplicity is almost gone. It might become a relic of a once innocent time, where people were saner and happier. But we all have a choice not to let this happen. We can choose to simplify our lives and begin to develop an intelligent relationship with technology. We have a unique opportunity to allow technological innovation to benefit our simplicity.

Chapter 2

The Benefit of Technological Innovation and the Dawn of the Digital World

We cannot doubt the positive impact technological innovation has had on our lives. I can write this book because the ancient Egyptians created the first pen (reed pen or reed brush) and Cai Lun (48-121 CE) of ancient China created paper. We can get from A to B much faster and more efficiently because of the car. We can travel all over the world because the Wright brothers' vision has become fully realized, something that before 1903 wasn't possible. Imagine your life without a refrigerator? It's hard to imagine life without it, or the oven, the faucet, and a host of other innovations that we don't consider technology. Just think of the heightened technological innovation to create a pen, a small invention that we overlook but when examined is revealed to have changed the course of human history because the pen is continually realized to be mightier than the sword.

A lot of small technological innovations we overlook because we lose sight of their impact and significance. But without paper, glass, silverware, doors, a sink, shower, toilet, electricity, and so on, we could not sit in the privileged position we are in today. I say privileged position because we live in a world now where it is much easier to reach our potential than ever before. All of the small incremental tech innovations for thousands of years have led to this point in time where we really have no more excuses for doing nothing productive or meaningful with our lives.

The sad reality is most people squander this potential because their time and energy is spent on frivolous entertainment and our modern obsession with watching other people's lives, usually who we believe are more successful. This trend leads to a generation of passive observers and not active participants. All of this privileged potential is squandered because we are too distracted and can't focus. But if you can harness all this tech innovation then you have the potential to make a positive impact in the world.

Technology Enhancing Our Lives

Our lives are better and more sustainable because of technological innovation. All of the technological innovation in agricultural methods has allowed us to feed most of the world (I am mindful that there is still a large population of people living in poverty, though the numbers have decreased slightly over time but it's nothing to get too excited about). Many people never have to skip a meal and obviously some take too much advantage of this convenience with growing rates in obesity.

But it's not just an abundance of food we have access to, it's also our comfortable home life that is enhanced. We have a comfortable bed to sleep in and highly efficient sanitation. Those old sanitation problems (often messy and stinky) are solved now with one push of the flush button. We don't have to hop, skip and jump our way through poo on the streets (sorry for being so graphic).

Most of the things we take for granted were once upon a time a laborious task. Take the simple invention of a faucet. Once upon a time we had to travel miles for water and now we just turn on the tap to drink some water, wash our clothes, and have a shower (though, in some nations people don't have the luxury of having a faucet in their homes and still have to travel miles for it). Most of us are privileged to have the faucet and we should be grateful because it took thousands of years of technological evolution to get it where it is today in its present state.

These simple innovations we take for granted have made our lives better. We are now in a position to reach our potential unencumbered. We have a unique choice to be conscious creators in this collaboration we call Earth. According to the late great psychologist Abraham Maslow, this ability to reach our full potential is only natural once all our basic needs are taken care of. In his psychological theory known as *Maslow's hierarchy of needs*, we begin to fulfill our creative urges and spiritual ideals easily once our needs are met. It's hard to argue with Maslow considering that once we have a stable environment, including shelter, access to food, clothing, and income, we begin to shift our focus to the higher aims of life which facilitates our ability to express the intrinsic beauty of life.

Without our basic needs met there would be no Bach, Picasso, Spielberg, Thurston, Jordan, Ronaldo, etc. Their art and athletic ability would never have eventuated. But thankfully their basic needs were met and they inspired the world as a result. And in a lot of their cases, they *just* had their basic needs met. They didn't need too much. Having more rather than less is an illusion modern culture promotes. Once the foundation of their lives was settled then the higher aims of human life came into view. This is only natural.

All of the blood, sweat, and tears spilt over the evolution of technology has allowed us to realize these intrinsic aims we have within. And because of all this technological innovation, it is much easier to be a creative person these days, as we have access to most of the means necessary to do so. But the irony is we live in a very uncreative world if we take into consideration that most of us squander our potential. Instead of being creative after our needs are met, we want more and more of everything as our greed consumes us.

Technology has freed our greed, as we can attempt to please most of our desires no matter whether they are positive or negative. We can either choose to reach our potential or to mooch off life. We need to ask ourselves if all this technological innovation that has improved our lives has come at a cost.

Better at What Cost?

In Steven Pinker's book *Enlightenment Now* (the same title as my book which he conveniently borrowed) he explains how our lives are improving. He shows a lot of analysis and statistics to prove his point. Personally, I love Pinker's view because it paints a more optimistic picture of the future of human civilization. Too often we are pessimistic about the future and cynical about human behavior. And yet here I am writing a book that may appear pessimistic about the world and where it is headed with digital technology. I am not lost on the irony. But bear with me and you will find an optimistic outlook after reading.

It is refreshing to see an esteemed person like Pinker not all *doom and gloom* about the world. He explains in his book that longevity, car crashes, child mortality, etc., have all improved. The media won't spread this great news, so thank God for Pinker. But one area Pinker doesn't overly address is the impact of our modern lifestyle on the natural world. He makes an argument that consumption is not entirely bad because it has allowed us to travel the world, be warmer in winter, and cool in summer. And he does have a point here, but he needs to recognize that these creature comforts are not common for everybody and are actually avoided by some people who are more conscious of their footprint (for example, I know many people who never use air conditioning no matter how hot it is). Also, these opportunities we have now to travel the world, for example, are small in comparison to the consumerist habits that have people perpetually buying shit they don't need, which is likely causing more damage to the environment than travel. Though, he somehow generalizes that people like to blame the other guy, but they say nothing about their own habits such as drinking fine wine. This is a sweeping generalization and he might be only speaking about his own circle of friends who can afford fine wine, or he could be referring to your average snob who has a righteous opinion but is out of touch with the real world and real people.

Yet, he is concerned about pollution, but he believes we don't need to rail against it. He suggests that countries become cleaner as they get richer. But as we've witnessed over time, the opposite is true. His optimism about overconsumption may be wishful thinking. And his optimism about consumption is avoiding the fact that it is our individual lifestyles that need to be transformed. This will happen when we understand our mind more and our desires less; then our consumerist habits will decrease. Yes, life is getting better but at what cost? Our lives have gotten better but we are out of sync with nature. Our modern lifestyle of excess has put an unnecessary strain on nature.

This lifestyle of excess has gone too far. If we continue down this path then we may want a one-way ticket with Elon Musk to Mars as his belief that we will outgrow and outsource this planet may one day come true (not to sound all doom and gloom). We don't have to consider such drastic measures if we can acknowledge that our lifestyle of excess is the problem. We have to simplify our lifestyle and that begins solely with you (something I will discuss at length in later chapters).

Desiring too much for our personal lives is destructive to nature. Though we don't personally see that impact doesn't mean it doesn't exist. We can't vicariously go on living the way we do. We have to acknowledge our modern lifestyle is the problem and we have the power to solve it any time we choose.

One of my friends used to say, "I must refuse my need to want." This could be a good mantra for us going forward. But we have to get out of the illusion that the "good life" is experienced when we have more than our needs. We are in a strange cycle of thinking that once our needs are met we should then focus on acquiring more material possessions as we build our personal empire. Most of us don't know this personal empire is truly a sandcastle. Modern culture advertises that this "more is better" attitude leads to the good life. It has everybody chasing their tails trying to climb over each other to be at the top of the heap. Most of us end up tied in knots as we suffer trying to get there.

Nobody considers an alternative to this epidemic. Not only is our greed destroying nature, it is also destroying ourselves (we are nature as well). We have to get out of this greed mindset and truly understand that *less is more*. Not only is this attitude of having less better for our relationship to nature, it is also better for us on a personal level because having less allows more space within our mind, leading to more creative and peaceful lives.

Having more complexifies our lives, leading to anxiety and shallowness. We consume, consume, consume, leaving a wasteland for future generations. The "more is better" attitude develops a shallow culture only interested in having more, which not only makes the planet a desert but also turns our vibrant traditional cultures into a cultural desert.

The irony is a lot of people are aware of their actions but they just can't help themselves. The appeal of having more is all-consuming. We believe that having more leads to better comfortability and convenience. But this is truly an illusion, especially when you examine our lack of happiness. Having less and living a simple life is more comfortable and convenient because we are naturally happier and our mind is more equanimous. When we are not chasing the mirage of success, we access our natural peace of mind. And this peaceful mind is not interested in the greed of modern culture.

If we all discovered this inner peace and tranquility it would be disastrous for Madison Avenue. But the advertising industry doesn't care about you or the environment so you shouldn't feel any sympathy. The advertising industry, which is a big part of modern culture, is not concerned about its impact on nature or the human mind. Advertising has hypnotized people to endlessly consume things they don't need. As a result, we are churning out waste at a speed that nature can't keep up with.

With our lives improving socially, we are ironically depleting nature and causing more waste than she is accustomed to handling. An extreme example is the Great Pacific garbage patch. It is an accumulation of plastic the size of three Frances located between the US and Japan. It is an ecological problem that everyone is avoiding. But just avoiding it because it is in "no man's land" doesn't mean it will go away. The technological benefits of plastic are coming back to bite us. But the irony is, even though technology created plastic, technology will be the reason why the Great Pacific garbage patch can be cleaned up and recycled. This is the benefit of technological innovation. And we can't really blame technology for something like the Great Pacific garbage patch because that is the result of human behavior. Our excessive behavior leads to these sorts of ecological problems.

We can't assume our lives are better if nature is harmed. But if we can learn to use technology wisely it will simplify our lives, which is one of the reasons technology was designed in the first place. Technology can be good for us if it is used to simplify our lives, freeing us to reach our full potential. But with the advent of the digital world, not only is simplicity lost, but technology has gone too far.

Dawn of the Digital Age

The dawn of the digital age has put the "technology is good for us" debate into question. Human beings are really simple creatures, though many people would believe we are not. But we truly are simple and herein lies the conflict with digital technology. Digital technology is this complex system that we superimpose on ourselves. We assume this will improve our lives and have no long-term effects. This book begs to differ as you will read in later chapters.

The long-term effects are ever so slowly eliminating the natural beauty of life. This could be viewed in many different ways. For example, a lot of digital technology produced these days, such as smartphones, doesn't even find a home and becomes rubbish. Not to mention the impact on the environment in producing all these digital gadgets. But digital technology is also eliminating the natural beauty of human life. We are so consumed by the digital world that we don't know what is going on around us. We rarely bump into a stranger at the subway and look each other in the eye and strike up a friendly conversation because our face is buried in our phone. People now walk with their face buried in their phone and they don't know what is happening in front of them, which is very dangerous.

We are losing touch with each moment. We are becoming desensitized to the natural world. We sit in a park or go for a walk in the bush but we don't hear the insects or experience the fresh air entering our lungs because the digital world is supposedly more appealing. Being truly present in the moment is being destroyed. We can't be fully present if we are distracted by what is in the digital world. It is amazing that when a noise comes from the phone our attention is completely distracted. Why? What is so appealing about the digital world?

We are missing out on so much because our nature is being suppressed by the digital world. Walking silently, peacefully, with no agitation in the mind is frightening for most people. We have to give our mind a toy to play with and social media is often its fix. This agitation in our mind is fueled by the digital world. And an agitated mind is something very common because most people seek distraction from being completely present or dealing with the brutal reality of their lives. The digital world has only multiplied this problem.

We are literally walking around out of our minds, as we delve into thoughts and imaginations stimulated by the digital world. We are not *here*, not present to experience the natural beauty of life. The digital world is guiding us away from that natural beauty. As a result, a human is losing their nature, the spontaneous nature at the core of our existence. Losing touch with our nature leads to a world gone insane. An insane world leans into distractions as opposed to refraining from them.

Chapter 3

Distracted People in an Insane World

Our world doesn't consider that we're distracted to the point of conscious sleep at the steering wheel of our own life. We've never considered that our minds are distracted. We don't think it is a problem. Actually, and also sadly, we don't even know our minds are distracted most of the day. We seek to be distracted and crave to be in that state of mind. People run away from a mind that is present and focused. This is not a recent phenomenon; it's been a persistent problem throughout the ages.

Spiritual practices, such as meditation, have sprung up to train our mind to be less distracted. But meditation hasn't been widely taken on as a daily practice, nor is it considered to counteract a distracted mind since people don't believe distraction is a problem. This is disastrous. How can we blame others or our culture for the state of the world if on an individual level we are not even present? The reason a lot of situations get out of hand is because the majority of people are out of their minds. They are literally swimming in their own thoughts, imagination, and the perpetual stories their minds ruminate on. This distracted state has only increased its potency in the modern world.

The reason why the world is lacking substance is because we are not present to imbue it with beauty. How can the world have substance if we are walking around mindlessly in our own personal stories in our head? It could not. With distractions increasing exponentially, where are we headed as a species? And why is our distracted state increasing exponentially? The reason for this is none other than the digital world. Digital technology is revealing our mental stupor, but thankfully it has exposed our addiction to distraction.

Addicted to Distraction

Socialization puts a lot of unnecessary pressure on the individual. The world is set up in such a way that we crave to distract ourselves from it because we really want to escape its clutches. The majority of us find ourselves in employment we tolerate at best, which consumes most of our time each day leaving us with not much energy to pursue our creative interests. So, we seek reprieve from the brutal reality of our meaningless jobs. But are our lives so gruesome that we truly need to seek distraction?

The good news is our lives are not so bad. We have the potential to change our lives at any moment, but it requires a change in orientation from wasting our time with distractions to cultivating focus and presence. More distractions won't get you out of an undesirable life situation. More focus and presence, which are characteristics of people who don't waste time, are needed. When we are more focused, we get more done. This is especially important if you want to create something that matters.

We have to cultivate focus and presence, and consciously avoid distracting ourselves. But most people are continually wasting the precious little time they have. You cannot change your current job or life situation if the spare time you have is wasted on distracting yourself. That doesn't mean you shouldn't have fun and enjoy yourself, but you have to become aware of the difference between enjoying yourself naturally and using your spare time to sedate yourself with distractions.

Sadly, we have become timewasters with no compass. As I've discussed, we live in a world now where a lot of our needs are taken care of but we squander this opportunity. This opportunity is the first of its kind, it is unique. But we don't know what to do with it. Our mind is free from a lot of the stress and burden put on us daily before the advent of a lot of technology. However, we are still exhibiting behavior that has an addictive quality. This is best represented through the use of digital technology. And a lot of older folks push this on to the attitude of millennials and iGen'ers but then you find all around the world elderly people clutching their digital devices.

When our life is a certain way that is out of sync with what we would like it to be, we begin to lean into addictions. This goes for all age groups. Addiction takes us away from the life we *have*. The more we can escape our life the more we will depend on addictions. Distraction itself is the common drug of choice. And the digital world is increasingly fulfilling our addictive tendencies. We are wasting the majority of our lives distracting ourselves. We spend most of our life in a state of sedation, without any sense of presence.

We all have the potential to shine in this world if we can pull up our bootstraps. It requires focus and a reevaluation of what is important in your life. What are the things you want to achieve and experience in this life? But, to live such a meaningful life, we have to refrain from the addictive qualities of distraction. We have to examine why we have become addicted to distraction. What is the source of this distraction that turns us into mere junkies seeking the next fix (or I should say seeking Netflix)?

Entertainment Junkies

Our primary source of distraction is entertainment. Entertainment pulls us out of our life and plants us in another reality. Our digital devices are a highway for entertainment to flow freely. Digital technology locks us into being entertained any spare moment we have. People have a firm grasp of their smartphone anywhere they go, and when there's an opportunity we dive deep into our smartphone when there's a spare moment to be entertained. Instead of waiting to get home to watch your favorite program on TV, you can just view it on your smartphone while you ride the subway, for example. This type of activity becomes a habit.

Slowly over time people went from looking each other in the eye and talking face to face in a restaurant and on the street, to staring at their smartphones. I find it quite sad when I go outside and see people mindlessly scrolling through their smartphones. Even when I go into nature people are busy getting a selfie of themselves to post instantly on Instagram. They are not truly present.

British philosopher Alan Watts once mentioned about how when he visited many tourist attractions in Japan most people were focused on getting photos to capture the experience but they weren't truly present to *really* experience the moment. Just imagine if Watts could see the world now, he might choke on his pipe. Anywhere we go now we are like the tourists in Japan in Watts' experience. We are either trying to document our own life or we are watching TV shows, movies, sports, or playing computer games.

I remember living in South Korea and one day I saw a couple in their 60s walking and the husband was staring into his smartphone and he stopped and told his wife to go ahead without him while he squatted on the sidewalk to continue his activity. I was curious about what was so important, and as I walked past, he was playing some sort of stupid ball game on his phone akin to Tetris. How could this be more important than enjoying the company of his wife? South Korea, though, is a bad example considering it is the most digitally connected place in the world. Computer games in South Korea are a big source of entertainment, where people can be distracted for hours on end and sometimes, if you can believe it, for days. PC gaming in South Korea has led to the adult diaper craze, as the gamers don't have time for a number two because they are busy conquering their imaginary world.

A tragic example is of a South Korean couple and their infant daughter. The couple had become obsessed with playing a role-playing game called Prius Online at an Internet café where they would raise a virtual daughter called Anima. Shockingly, they would leave their *real* infant daughter unattended while they were at the Internet café. They would occasionally drop by to feed her powdered milk. One day, after a 12-hour gaming session, they returned home to find their three-month-old daughter dead. She had starved to death. They had neglected their real daughter's health for some fake daughter they created in a world that doesn't exist. I know this is extreme, but this is the world we live in. And it's not only a problem in South Korea, but now the entire world.

It doesn't matter what source of entertainment it is, because we are junkies clinging to our next fix. Over-entertaining ourselves is such a bad habit and no one wants to address the problem. It is a taboo topic, but it is imperative to understand this addiction if we want a healthy and sane world.

Any spare time we have we want to entertain ourselves and sadly not *know* ourselves. We waste so much time entertaining ourselves that it outweighs what we actually achieve for ourselves in our daily life. People often wonder why their lives are the way they are and why nothing good has happened for them. But many of us don't want to acknowledge that we are timewasters and this habit builds momentum when we become accustomed to being distracted.

It is not possible for us to be creative and productive if we are constantly distracted by entertainment. Recall your last week and calculate the amount of time you wasted on a digital screen and then calculate the amount of time you were creative. For the majority of people the former outweighs the latter tenfold (this obviously doesn't apply to those who are creative in the digital world).

We need to reclaim our time. In doing so, we will ignite our creativity. But we have to make a conscious decision to refrain from entertainment. If we don't, we will continue to waste time and essentially waste our lives. We've all surely noticed that when we are online, how innocently opening an e-mail can lead to visiting another website or falling down the rabbit hole of YouTube and then next thing we know four hours have vanished, nothing achieved but an anxious memory of lost time. We can easily stop ourselves from this sort of habit, but as with any addiction we lose ourselves because we can't help ourselves.

People binge for hours on end with entertainment. We will discover a TV series and binge on it day after day. In some cases, people will finish an entire season of *Game of Thrones* in one sitting. This is complete madness. Being constantly distracted has desensitized us. Our natural response when we are wasting time is to get anxious because deep down, we know we should be doing something creative or productive, something worthwhile. But this response is beginning to be turned off, which is evident in the fact that someone could actually watch a whole TV series in one day. We are completely lost in the stories in our head, which entertainment helps to fuel. If it wasn't already bad enough that the mind wanders in its own delusion that now it has entertainment as rocket fuel to deal with.

We watch so much entertainment that our mind begins to ruminate on the fictional stories we've been watching. When we start to dream about what we watch then we know we've gone too far. But there seems to be no end in sight. The shows and movies we can binge on keep coming and coming, taking us far away from our own lives. Instead of living a wonderful and adventurous life, we watch someone else's version of it. We could invest in our own life but it is easier to watch someone else do all the great things for us. Instead of binging on entertainment, we should invest our time and energy into knowing what makes us truly tick. But truly knowing oneself requires knowledge and sustained effort. That sort of commitment is frightening for most, especially if it cuts into our distraction time.

We are scared to look within ourselves because we are frightened of what we might find. It's easier to hold up an image of ourselves (especially on social media) that represents the person we think we should be. We find it easier to express ourselves to some degree rather than knowing our deep-down nature. This is what makes social media so appealing. We can just document a positive version of ourselves while trying to pretend we don't have any problems, or in a troll's case, above anyone else's opinion.

By ignoring our own inner nature, we create a new social media ego that is either all gooey and positive or all self-righteous and arrogant. In many cases we are recreating ourselves into who we wish we truly were. But the reality is we are not that social media ego. And I can tell you from my years being an author and teacher that some of the people I've met face to face from social media are not who they truly portray, some being bitter and others just plain assholes (though I have mainly met wonderful people from social media, which probably says more about the level of maturity of my audience due to the nature of my content). Keep in mind, it is hard for social media to give an accurate assessment of who you truly are. It truly can't. It might be able to express some view you have, or wish you had, but it can't tell your story accurately. But that doesn't stop a troll, as their whole sad life is built on semantics and stupidity (a bit more on that in the next chapter).

As a result of all of the above, social media has become a source of entertainment, maybe the most destructive of all. People are constantly scrolling their Facebook or Twitter feeds viewing other people's lives as they compare their own lives to them. We are so inquisitive; we want to peer into other people's lives which years ago might be called invasion of privacy. But the difference between now and then is we are actively putting our lives out there for the whole world to see. And the way the world is now, it seems more important how our social media network appears than our actual *real* life. As a result, our neck begins to lean forward in an unnatural position, as our eyes are fixed on our digital screens. It's hard to view people acting in this way and not think that this is the zombie apocalypse. Well, it might not be at that stage yet, but creating a digital ego and our attraction to shows and computer games, for example, are all new adaptations that have created the mindless crowd.

The Mindless Crowd

These adaptations keep the crowd tuned to the same beat. I remember living in Seoul traveling the subway watching the majority of the crowd walking the same fast speed as they stare into their smartphones. This same vision I witnessed traveling the subway in New York and the tube in London and many other places around the world. It is like a global march of the flies and it is hard not to be cynical and think that we are living amongst zombies. But we are not zombies, even though our movements are beginning to replicate a zombie. We are humans, though many of us have forgotten.

What is concerning, though, is we are exhibiting the traits of a mindless crowd. We are walking around mindlessly and not present to what is actually happening around us. We are engaged in our screens or have our headphones on listening to something. We are not present. Everything is taking us far away from the immediate moment.

Being present in the immediate moment is something we want to be taken away from. We need to be distracted at all times. This is the essence of mindlessness. You are not present but rather you are in another imaginary reality. What you watch or listen to from your smartphone when you move around, for example, keeps your mind distracted from what you are experiencing, hence mindless. Our mind was not designed to navigate in such a complex manner, it is a terrible multitasker even though it can clumsily multitask. And yet, people the world over are mimicking this multitasking attitude. As I mentioned, it's all to the same beat.

You can view the world over and there seems to be this sameness of activity with rarely anything unique. When people begin to mimic the actions and attitudes of each other, then the mindless crowd is formed. For me, it's like a horror film when I'm in a public place and people are all engaged with their digital devices. I feel a deep sadness when I'm in a restaurant and see a couple or a family all clutching their smartphones, completely disconnected from one another. What is so important in the digital world that can't wait? We all know the answer is nothing special, but people are addicted to their smartphones and lose interest in life itself.

What is so interesting about our phones that we will substitute mindlessness for life? The answer again is nothing special. This is evident in the fact that there is not much diversity in what people consume through the digital world. The content is very similar. People are either scrolling social media, watching shows or sport, reading gossip, and in summary, people are just watching other people's lives from a distance.

Watching other people's lives while not investing in your own life is such a terrible habit. This is what separates those on the stage (anyone well-known) to those in the crowd (the rest of us). The people on the stage are focused on their own lives and in some cases being a better person. The people in the crowd are interested in watching successful people from a distance, so they can either shower those people with unnecessary adulation or tear them down with cynicism. Not to discredit or take away anything from those on the stage, but you need to stop watching people and focus on becoming a better person so that one day you are on the stage and not part of the mindless crowd (keep in mind *stage* here means someone who is not distracted and has done something with their lives).

The reason why people in the crowd don't strive to be better is because they are not *present* in their own life. How could you be a better version of yourself if you are constantly watching other people be better versions of themselves? This is the attitude of the mindless crowd. The digital world is promoting this attitude. But this is not only what the digital world is doing. It is also revealing the deep-seated mental state of the mindless crowd that builds the psychology within the digital world.

Part II

The Digital World is Destroying the Mind

Chapter 4

The Psychology of the Digital Mind

Has humanity gone to the point of no return? Can we be saved from our materialistic habits that are increasingly destroying nature? Can we be saved from identification with group mentality which only contributes to a world increasingly divided? It appears that our mind is so polluted that it is not possible for people to realize their true nature. Humanity is like a freight train with no brakes.

This is a grim view shared by many and it's one we have to consider. But I'm optimistic about our future even though I can sympathize with this grim view, as you can tell with this book. We have not considered the average mental state of humanity because we believe everything is fine and dandy. We believe the psychological health of the average individual is nothing to worry about. But nothing could be further from the truth.

We've never truly known the magnitude of our psychological problems. That is until now. The digital world is revealing the deep-seated problems people have but have never been expressed. Social media has especially facilitated these problems. Facebook, Twitter, YouTube, Instagram, hell even LinkedIn, have given birth to a new form of species in the digital evolution, trolls.

The Birth of Trolls

I remember when I had my first book coming out and I had no social media accounts. This was the end of 2010. Before that I had a few forays into Facebook and YouTube but I never lasted. I just thought they were all a waste of time. I never knew what Twitter and LinkedIn were and Instagram was not around at the time. My wife and I had been traveling all through Asia and Africa from 2008 to 2010, so we missed the memo on smartphones and its relationship to social media.

To our shock horror, when we arrived back in Australia in 2010, we noticed people had begun to forget about face-to-face contact as their faces were buried in their phone. Instantly I was put off by this relationship of social media in a phone. So, I have refrained from it. My first smartphone was reluctantly purchased in 2013 in Seoul because I needed a phone for teaching English and South Korea don't sell good old-fashioned button phones. But that smartphone was secondhand and it didn't have social media on it. I have basically turned it into an alarm clock and it can receive phone calls (that is when I have a phone number) but I prefer e-mail if you need to contact me. But it better be an emergency if you want to ring me because I'm busy living (thankfully that smartphone was completely useless being an older smartphone).

I wasn't aware about the impact of the smartphone and social media relationship, and how apparently important it is to people's lives. That is until the end of 2010 when the publisher of my first book was flabbergasted that I didn't have any social media presence. I didn't realize how crucial social media had become for marketing, especially if you are an author. So, I reluctantly bent to the will of my publisher.

I love writing and I am especially passionate about what I write about, so I was willing to make that sacrifice to get published. I uncomfortably created accounts with all the important social media networks. I felt like Alice falling down the rabbit hole. I was so fresh and naive that I didn't know what to expect. I naturally assumed the community was going to be like real life. But then reality hit. I was doing what anyone else was doing. I was posting and putting up videos about my work and creating intelligent discussions about what matters in human life. And then, as my work began to become more popular, I continued to come across a digital species that I couldn't understand, the basement-dwelling creatures known as trolls. Though I didn't know people called them trolls at the time. I naively assumed people would be well-mannered and engage in intelligent dialogue on social media. Oh, how I was wrong.

When I first encountered these sorts of unintelligent dialogues in reaction to my posts and videos, I didn't know how to deal with them. Any sane person didn't know to begin with. First of all, I didn't know these people other than a name on a screen. When I started to receive comments that were not intelligent and ridiculously critical and off-topic, I reacted naturally calm how anyone would in the real world, explaining my post more clearly to them, which resolves conflict in the real world. But then I began to learn that the unnatural environment of the digital world is not the same as the real world. I learned like anyone else, the hard way.

I realized a troll is not really interested in an intelligent discussion or hearing your opinion and knowledge. But instead, their aim is to bait you in a way similar to schoolboy tactics, just like your average bully. Yet a troll is way more vicious than innocent schoolboys. They will throw all sorts of wild accusations your way to try and bait you, and if you are not aware of what they are doing then they'll end up depleting your energy from a meaningless exchange.

This cycle of insanity gets worse the more popular you become. In the ten-plus years I've put my work out there on social media, the increase in troll activity has tripled as my work has become more popular. With that comes more unintelligent dialogue and ridiculous accusations. One example is of a person who was criticizing me for taking people on sacred tours around India. My tour is called the *Footsteps of the Masters Tour*, where I take people to some of the most sacred places in India. People get to travel to the famous Bodhi tree where the Buddha became enlightened, the holy mountain of Arunachala, and many UNESCO sites such as in Mahabalipuram.

Many people have benefited from my tour. But when I was promoting this tour a person on Facebook started saying that she would never go on this tour because of all the crimes of sex with children in India. She was implying that I support this sort of crime because I travel to India. I, mistakenly, tried to explain to her that this is a global problem, it doesn't just happen in India (sane people know this, but it's hard for a troll to comprehend). I explained how wonderful and innocent the majority of the Indian people are and how their culture is amazing and how we can all learn a lot from them. She shockingly called me a pedophile because she said that anyone who travels India is a supporter of such criminal activity (she was also very racist and had a low opinion of Indian people in her outburst). I was shocked and saddened that someone who doesn't know me could just say something so disgusting and not be punished for it.

What made me angry about this situation is this troll's psychological problem made my wife upset. Just think how you would feel if some insane person made up stuff about someone you love? In the real world they would be called out and rightfully condemned. But in the digital world you can be this sort of keyboard assassin and get away with it scot-free. We can be charged for false accusations in the real world. So why should the digital world be any different? Why should my wife and I have to put up with such pain while that troll moves on to the next person to bait? Why did Facebook not protect us from such attacks? Shouldn't they hold trolls accountable for their actions?

These immature actions gave birth to "call-out culture," which is rife on social media (basically the seed of cancel culture). Call-out culture is where people will interpret a social media post in their own way and then accuse the person of being a bigot, religious fundamentalist, racist, nationalist, etc. This is evidence as to why social media is hard to convey what someone is truly trying to express, because people misinterpret things online due to their own biases and agendas. And when this misinterpretation begins with incorrect accusations, then the gang mentality begins with no concern for the mental health of the person you are cowardly ganging up on. The effect of this cowardice behavior over time is people are afraid to speak their mind which sadly stops the free flow of ideas leading to real progress, not the absurd "progressiveness" of call-out culture and their troll in numbers mentality.

In the real world we are held accountable for our actions. It's called sanity. A sane person does not act insane, but an insane person should learn accountability for their actions. But this common sense is not practiced in the digital world. So, for someone like myself, I naturally got stronger and refused to engage with trolls. If I get a hint of a conversation heading in that direction I will just disengage. Trolls waste too much precious time and energy.

These sorts of petty strategies employed by trolls are being exploited on a much larger scale than just personal attacks on people like myself. Successful online troll behavior has been noticed for its effectiveness in causing dissent among the general population. Countries such as Russia have especially paid attention to the effectiveness of troll behavior. They've taken this phenomenon to the next level with highly organized troll farms (though, state-sponsored sock puppetry and manipulation of online views is also practiced by several other countries, in particular the United States, United Kingdom, China, Israel, Turkey, Iran, Vietnam, and Ukraine).

Troll farms are strategically used to cause conflict within certain populations around the world. The most obvious example is the influence Russian troll farms had on the 2016 US presidential election. Unbeknown to most Americans, Russian troll farms were online wreaking havoc. They were fueling conflict online, using people's political orientation as gasoline. Thousands of fake social media accounts were inciting arguments between Americans with opposite views, using political and sexual orientation, religion, race, gender, etc., to cause unnecessary conflict (Twitter released to Congress 10 million tweets that had been circulated by propaganda farms[1]). And these fake accounts are widespread online. You've probably experienced it as well. I'm not sure why ordinary people like you and me would be in the crosshairs of a troll farm, but we have to remember the goal of a troll farm is just to cause conflict, with seemingly no preference towards one group or another. Personally, I'm always receiving friend requests on Facebook from accounts that are very suspicious. When I have inspected some of these accounts, they'll just have a profile picture with no posts. I will just decline this request and mark it as spam if it is extremely suspicious.

YouTube, on the other hand, is a little more difficult to monitor. I get a lot of comments on my videos from accounts that have no subscribers and an odd assortment of videos they've liked and some with no likes at all. These accounts usually return to other videos of mine writing comments that are out of context with the video content or they try to cause an argument with a real user. I'm not sure why a troll farm employee would be interested in little ol' me; maybe they were bored or maybe I am just too suspicious of this type of online activity. Or maybe this is just the general sanity of a troll. Nevertheless, troll farms exist and their core objective of inciting social unrest is not in your best interest.

I have plenty of friends who will just add any account that requests their friendship. Then the troll goes to work on trying to influence them one way or another, usually using conflict to really fuck-up their day. Be aware of such activity and don't engage. No matter whether it is a troll farm or a slimy troll working solo, they want your attention so your best bet is to ignore them which sucks the life out of their miserable existence.

With the birth of trolls, the helpless grim view of the world held by many appears right. We are truly in bad shape. Shame on all you trolls for proving this grim view correct, get your act together. We are humans, not monkeys (I'm sorry to offend monkeys as a representation of a troll). But the troll is still a young species and not properly understood. To understand this digital creature, we have to ask if these are preexisting deep-seated psychological problems or are they how people would truly act if social cues were taken away? Or is it a mix of both? Is this how we would act from a distance if there were no repercussions?

The Troll Mind

In the real world most people are relatively well-mannered. We don't go out of our way to cause trouble. It is rare to see people arguing with each other, at least in an unintelligent manner. We've all witnessed people who know each other get into it an argument over something important they both know about. It would be unique if a stranger started arguing with you on the street regarding things they don't really know about but they just verbally attack you because they can do that. That would be insane, but this is the environment in the digital world that we are supposed to tolerate.

That act of insanity is the psychology of a troll. They depend on unintelligent personal attacks, as most of the time a troll doesn't know their victim personally. They feel a sense of safety in being a keyboard assassin, because the likelihood of ever confronting that troll is miniscule. But are trolls exhibiting how we would truly act if all the rules, regulations, and accepted manner were taken away? Is all this social pleasantness just a facade? Are we just trained animals? The answer is no. I've lived in countries that don't have many rules and regulations and people still treat each other well. Actually, in most cases people treat each other better without all of these rules and regulations choking them.

We could also say the answer is no because the majority of people on the Internet act civilized when social cues are not present. But the problem with this answer is the troll mentality is growing and good people are developing bad habits. This troll mentality is not isolated to people we would call pests or parasites. Good and decent people are falling victim to troll habits.

People are slowly becoming comfortable with being mischievous when there are no filters and no accountability for their actions. Behaving like this from a distance is a problem. Even in Confucius's time, he warned us about how we act when we are alone because a lot of us act one way when social cues are needed and another way when no one is looking. His point is we usually let our demons run amok when no one is watching us. This means there are deeper factors at play that reveal themselves from the comfort of anonymity. Acting in this manner reveals our deep-seated psychological problems.

Our afflictions have always been within. But instead of addressing them, we project them onto others. And this goes from the gross troll view of violent verbal abuse ranging from bigotry and racism to death threats, to the subtlety of unfounded personal attacks on one's character. This sort of abuse is rife in the comments section on social media. This sort of behavior is usually found in the comments section of posts or videos from inspired people doing something valuable with their lives.

Tearing people down is common in ordinary chitchat, but it is at its worst online. Even the gossipiest person will refrain from being racist or wish people death in the real world. But not the troll, nothing is too sacred. A troll's targets are usually people doing great things in their lives, successful people. This behavior is a deep-seated problem within many people. People tear other people down because they themselves feel inadequate. You know the cynical phrase, "Who does she think she is?" This is usually uttered because the successful individual is actually doing something positive with their life and the one slandering them is jealous and feels inadequate because they are wasting their life.

If you are someone doing something positive with your life don't be surprised where such negativity comes from, even behind your back in the real world. I've had family and friends act in this cynical way behind my back, but of course not face to face. This is the luxury reserved for a troll in the digital world. In either world the problem is the same, but just expressed more freely in the digital world because of anonymity. It is quite immature to attack someone to make ourselves feel better in our uneventful life.

An alien from another world would assume humans on Earth hate success and sharing well wishes with those who do good in the world. Our feelings of envy, jealousy, and inadequacy are fueled by our negativity bias. Negativity bias is the psychological term referring to our evolutionary habit to focus more so on negative events even if they are small in comparison to positive events. An unhealthy diet of verbal cynicism is a main contributor to the negativity bias that has evolved in our brains. Psychology offers a definition:

> The negativity bias refers to the notion that, even when of equal intensity, things of a more negative nature (e.g. unpleasant thoughts, emotions, or social interactions; harmful/traumatic events) have a greater effect on one's psychological state and processes than neutral or positive things.[2]

We all feel negativity bias within us. It's what leads us into cynicism and why gossip feels so comfortable for most people. We love when famous people slip-up because we can gossip behind their back making us feel "good." We live in a culture fueled by the negativity bias, hence why the news is so popular.

The news fuels our cynicism, as it continues to stimulate our envy, jealousy, and hatred for others.

This negative culture has entered the realm of social media leading to the evolution of the troll mind. A troll succumbs to negativity bias and, as a result, they freely exercise their cynicism. They believe it makes them feel good. But they are only avoiding the psychological problems they have. A troll's target, someone doing something valuable with their lives, are the people who have made the choice to better themselves and not succumb to cynicism or hatred. For all of you with troll tendencies, instead of being cynical try sending your best wishes and be supportive. This type of positivity might feel painful to begin with, but it's one of the only methods to blunt our negativity bias and also address our psychological problems.

You have no reason to feel inadequate if you are truly content in your own life. Discontent is not the result of someone else doing something with their lives, but instead the reality that you are wasting your life and squandering your potential. It comes down to the inner work we all need to do. A troll is just someone who succumbs to their own problems. They then project these problems onto others to try and bring them down to their level. But even though a troll may engage you online into their own bullshit, you are still not at their petty level and your only problem was engaging with them in the first place.

To fix this problem we need to start feeding the good wolf within us. This will begin the long overdue inner transformation on to a healthy and sane life. This wolf analogy is especially important when referring to troll mentality. Not just trolls, but also people in general succumb to feeding the bad wolf, which is the bad habit of regressing into negativity. When we constantly feed the bad wolf, the good wolf is starved of nutrition. We can only feed the good wolf when we say *no* to our negativity bias and instead embrace a positive view of life and other people. Instead of being a keyboard assassin, try being a keyboard well-wisher. You will feel much better.

Continually feeding the bad wolf is a weakness. This weakness is a troll's fuel. None of us have to stoop so low, we can embrace our good wolf to make a positive impact. This choice is the indication that you love the world rather than oppose it. When there are no social cues and anonymity the bad wolf in us wants to be mischievous and cause unwanted drama. We need to stop feeding the bad wolf and put our energy into the good wolf.

Our lives are often a representation of which wolf we've been feeding most of our lives, and this goes also for those of us who are the targets of trolls. We can often be engaged in a troll's bullshit and this leads us to invariably feed the bad wolf in self-defense. Not all of us are in the privileged position of heavyweight boxing champion Deontay Wilder. Wilder had the unique opportunity to face one of his trolls with boxing gloves on in the gym. Obviously, this was a mismatch. Wilder gave the troll a few explosive punches and the troll basically shit his pants. Those few punches definitely woke the troll out of his slumber. But not all of us have that opportunity, nor do I condone that sort of violence. So, the best way for you to deal with trolls is to work on yourself, to go through an inner transformation (this advice is also for a troll as well).

You need to develop mental muscle to not engage with trolls. You have to stop defending yourself, because if what a troll says about you is nonsense then why bother defending yourself (in Part III I will explain strategies for not engaging with trolls). Developing your mental muscle will give you the strength to transform yourself to reclaim your natural humanness. Losing our humanity is an outcome of succumbing to the troll mind. But we also lose our humanity from dwelling too much in the digital world. We are increasingly isolating ourselves from each other, so it is no surprise we don't understand each other. This began ever so slowly with technology.

Distorted Human Interaction

We are closed off from each other. Living in our own little world fuels troll mentality. Our isolation distorts our perception. People look out into the world and only see a threat to our little way of life. Technology has caused a lot of this isolation. Television began this process. We started to stay home more and stare into the idiot box. This might have appeared innocent at first glance, but this did start the beginning of the end of community in the traditional sense.

Television began to be more appealing than going out and mingling with the world. This was the building blocks of a distortion in human interaction. But television's impact is miniscule compared to the functionality of mobile phones and the Internet. Having a mobile phone in your pocket, or anywhere on you, is a virus for human interaction.

Back in 2006 I noticed the impact of mobile phones and this was just with texting. I was at a bus stop going to work and everybody would dive into their phone while waiting for the bus. I noticed that nobody wanted to run the risk of making eye contact or having a conversation with a stranger (I'd probably avoid me too if I could). Most of the time back then people were pretending to do something on the phone but they were in reality only reading an old text, checking the time, or pretending to text someone to avoid conversation. This has got 100 times worse since smartphones were introduced.

The digital world cuts us off from natural interaction. We would prefer to communicate with people from a distance, or as it seems. People are starting to lose their natural intuitive sense in face-to-face contact. We are losing our sense of picking up subtle nuances in face-to-face interaction. People who spend way too much time in the digital world lose sense of subtle social cues and emotions. As a result, we become rude and lack the ability to be in the other person's shoes.

Human natural interactive skills are diminishing, especially with millennials and iGen'ers who have grown up with digital technology. I've witnessed many situations with millennials, iGen'ers and adults from older generation groups, where two people just can't understand each other nor reconcile their differences, and the result is they walk away from each other as if it isn't important at all. It's as if we are utilizing the "crop and delete" computer tool in real life.

People are sadly developing this crop and delete tendency. Anything or anyone that conflicts with our point of view or way of life we just crop and delete as if it or they don't exist. The people of this digital generation don't want to be disturbed. We want to remain in our delusion and illusion as we push the real world away. These isolated tendencies have created a culture with no humanness. Real interaction sustains humaneness because we can learn and grow from each other naturally.

A world lacking humanity is always annoyed by the world. If we go back to my bus stop example, just imagine you started talking to one of those people playing with their phones. The response would be, at least in their mind, "What does this person want?" They would have a feeling of being disturbed and annoyed. How dare you cut into their Facebook time. People always seem put out when you try to enter their isolated digital world.

The First World could learn a lot from the Third World on this matter of natural human interaction (though I personally don't consider the Third World lesser than the First World). India is a great example of keeping their humanity intact. In India it is common for people to look each other in the eye and talk to strangers.

One of my favorite pastimes is to go to an outdoor tea shop in India and watch the world go by. I have witnessed on many occasions the beauty of complete strangers interacting with each other as if they were long-lost friends. I've witnessed this many times firsthand. I've had Indian men and women come and sit with my wife and I and they start talking to us like we were long-lost friends. In most cases, these random conversations were much more innocent, pure, and fruitful than with a lot of people I know personally. The interactions are much more heartfelt.

India, and other less developed nations, have kept this natural interaction alive, even though they have access to phones. But community is much more important to them than living in digital isolation. This comes down to many factors. Nations such as India have more of a traditional culture which binds the people together. Plus, a big factor is their culture is built on a function of cognition that is holistic which hardly exists in the West (I will speak about this in the next chapter).

Having no *real* human interaction has deep psychological effects. In digital isolation we could care less about the world and it begins to show. We lose our ability to empathize, forgive, and be compassionate. We feel comfortable vicariously watching the world eat off each other. This is all done in the preservation and self-interest of the individual. Natural human interaction could not survive in such an individualistic digital world because our natural intuitive faculty is starved of oxygen. The digital world promotes self-interested individualism and this affects our naturalness. This all happens because our world is hellbent on focusing only on one function of cognition that naturally gravitates towards digital technology.

Chapter 5

Rationality is Killing the Mind

Our attraction to the analytical functionality of digital technology is in part the result of our cognitive training. The entire world is focused on training one cognitive function of the mind: the cold cognition. As I mentioned in Chapter 1, the cold cognition is the cognitive control centers located in the prefrontal cortex (PFC) in the frontal lobe of the brain. The function of the cold cognition is slow, effortful, and physiologically expensive. This is the analytical mind, the home of rationality. Our world in general doesn't know the terminology, but every nation unknowingly trains the cold cognition and suppresses the hot cognition. Hot cognition is the spontaneous, intuitive, and natural side of ourselves that does the majority of the work even though "I" as the cold cognition believe "I" am in control.

The world's education system is built on cold cognitive training. Fun and play become secondary and a minor part of our school days, as we find with physical education (PE is a lame attempt to keep children active). As a result, we are turned into human calculators. We become primarily analytical and lose our natural intuitive sense (hot cognition). Being primarily rational causes an imbalance in our cognition. We have overcompensated for cold cognition and this is why we feel the analytical view of rationality is the Holy Grail. Nothing could be further from the truth.

The Mind-Body Split and Embodied Cognition

Rationality is held as the Holy Grail since the Enlightenment movement in Europe and its colonies, where reason is assumed to trump all. This view has intensified in the modern world through education and how society judges intelligence. But this view is much older than the Enlightenment and we can't be too sure when it started. Yet we can trace some of its origins from the myth that being over rational produces: the *disembodied myth*.

The disembodied myth is a philosophical hangover from Plato down to influential philosophers such as Descartes and Immanuel Kant. These three philosophers played a significant role in propelling forward a dualistic model of mind and body based on vague intuitions they had about people who have minds and the physical world which, according to them, doesn't. This way of thinking developed the myth of mind-body dualism, the illusion that cold and hot cognition are separate and not integrated holistically.

Mind-body dualism is what we've all been indoctrinated with. We act as though we are this rational mind lugging around this completely irrational body. A subtle example of this is how we often say, "I had to drag myself out of bed this morning." This phrase is just plain weird. Who is dragging who out of bed? There is only one of you. The reason we assume there is another is because we, the "I," only identify with our cold cognition. We feel as though the body is some sort of lazy brute. For "us" in the cold cognition it is laborious to lug around this natural beast.

We all feel this split within us which is evident in our language and actions. Mind-body dualism has become the standard for us to understand ourselves and experience the world. Yet this is a myth because we are not disembodied entities exhibiting a sort of abstract rationality where reason is king. But rather our cognition is fundamentally *embodied*, where the mind is embodied and the body is mindful. This is the Eastern view of mind-body *holism*. We've all suffered from this split, even science. Science was also the victim of the disembodied myth until recently. Cognitive scientists in the mid-twentieth century treated the human mind as a brain in a container. Many experiments were concerned with abstract information processing which led them nowhere. It wasn't until the past few decades that cognitive science began to change its perspective.

Cognitive science is slowly moving away from the disembodied dualistic model and instead is beginning to treat human thought as fundamentally embodied. This means our thinking, even our abstract concepts, are grounded in concrete experiences that are linked to our bodily experiences through analogy and metaphor. Embodied cognition, then, as opposed to the disembodied view, ties thought inherently to feeling.

The rigid distinction between emotion and rationality is being brought into question by cognitive science. And this contributes significantly to the science of cultivating skill because cognitive scientists are starting to discover that the human brain is primarily designed for guiding action rather than a vehicle for representing abstract information. Yet the human brain can represent abstract information if it is required.

Embodied cognition is brought to light especially through *dual process theory* (the two systems of cognitive function). Hot and cold cognition are not two different entities jostling for pole position. They are fundamentally integrated. Both lead us to health, sanity, and well-being if we allow both to function naturally. The split implanted in us is not our conscious choice, but instead is the result of an entire world willing to sell their innate naturalness (hot cognition) for rationality (cold cognition) just so we can climb the social ladder of "success." Education and the digital world enhance this split.

Rational Training, Artificial Being

I've taught English to Chinese and South Korean school students. Nowhere in the world have I witnessed strict military-style education than in those two nations. To give you some context, my wife, who is Korean, in high school would go to school from 7am to 11pm. During this 16-hour period there is no letup, it is go, go, go and then more go.

In Far Eastern Asia this militarized rote learning begins very young. I've taught children as young as 2 and 3 years old and all they want to do is play, but their parents force them to listen to me in class, so it is very common for them to cry (I often felt more like a kindergarten teacher than an English teacher). This trend goes all the way up until they go to university. Parents will force their children into all sorts of private classes outside of their school classes. It's not uncommon for children in Far Eastern Asia to have private classes after school each day and both days on the weekend. It's constant rational training. There is no break.

Children are forced to be in their head (cold cognition) all the time. The side effects of such training are disastrous. As I mentioned in Chapter 1, South Korea has one of the highest rates of teen suicide because children, and especially teenagers, find it hard to breathe with too much rational training. There is no time for the naturalness of play (hot cognition).

The entire world believes rational training is more important than play. This is causing innumerable psychological problems leading to an artificial state of being. Focusing only on cold cognitive training (rationality) warps our nature. It causes a disturbance between the natural allocation of energy of the hot and cold cognition. Hot cognition is the bedrock of cold cognition. Hot cognition actually nourishes intellectual life (cold cognition) when it is accessed. If we don't play and relax, our subconscious has no time to work out intellectual problems we may have. Over employing cold cognition to solve an intellectual problem is like bashing your head against the wall hoping an answer will come to mind. Our cold cognition cannot be nourished and function optimally if we have no time to relax and play. This goes for anyone, no matter what age. But our nature is warped from a young age due to rational training.

This disturbance between both cognitive functions affects

our natural physical movements. Hot cognition controls our natural physical movements as well as expert skill. Opening and closing our hand, for example, is a hot cognitive function that is spontaneous and something we don't have to think about. This is the same for all our natural physical movements. Too much rational training causes a disequilibrium in our cognitive functions. Being in our head too much causes incoordination (for someone uncoordinated we use the slang term *unco* in Australia and New Zealand).

I've witnessed firsthand that Chinese and Korean students exposed to over rational training start to have trouble with natural physical tasks, forget about ones that require an element of skill. Just simple physical movements like jumping and running appear awkward. There is a lack of trust in their innate physical naturalness and a disharmony with nature's environment. When I first met my wife, she also struggled with trusting her natural movements. In our first years as a couple we were in the Himalayas trekking over some tricky terrain. I was bouncing from boulder to boulder with slow balanced steps. But my wife had to sit down and basically worm her way from boulder to boulder. I used to ask her why she doesn't trust her body. It confused me at the time because I didn't know what I know now. For myself, this was the benefit of growing up playing sport and always being outdoors (though I probably wasn't in my head enough growing up). My wife, on the other hand, grew up primarily in her head and behind her desk making her a lot smarter than I am. But her problem was that she was not adapted to the natural world (this has changed for her in recent times from years of exercise and being in nature). But this is not only a problem in Far East Asia; it has become a problem all around the world.

Training only cold cognition while eliminating play reduces our capacity to trust our organism to adapt to the natural terrain. Sitting at our desk and behind our computers all day destroys our relationship to nature on a deep cognitive level. We can't trust our body because we've been primarily in our cold cognition, where our overthinking separates the mind from the body. This leads to incoordination and no feel for nature's terrain.

A stark contrast to Far East Asia's over rational training is India. India is a country fully alive and definitely not a dull place (though a lot of people think differently without ever visiting there). Indian yogi and mystic Sadhguru best explained India as a forest rather than a manicured garden. What he meant by this sentiment is Indian culture and the people are wild in the best possible way because they understand that life is not certain. This means that India grows naturally and is not exhausted or depleted from trying to maintain a clean garden (rationality). Actually, the Hindu culture (along with other Eastern traditions) leans into hot cognition rather than trying to suppress it. Hence, their philosophies and spirituality are holistic based rather than individualistic. This affects Indian people at their core.

In general, Indian people have a good balance between hot and cold cognition. As a result, they are more at ease than other nationalities. Their ability to communicate, then, is at a higher level. Hence, people in India like to get out and about and mingle, which showcases a real sense of community other countries lack. All of this begins at a young age.

Indian children are often thrust into adult society at a very young age. For many children this is because of poverty, but for others it's because that is just the way life is in India. As a result, many Indian children grow naturally with the environment. Some cynics may believe that children from First World nations have higher IQ (intelligence quotient) scores than Indian children (though there are no statistics to support such a cynical claim). This might be the case per capita since India is a massive population (though, again this is just speculation), but they are vastly more intelligent emotionally and socially because many Indian children grow up quite young.

Keep in mind that having a high IQ score doesn't imply complete intelligence, as this is only an indication of how good one's cold cognitive training is, not how naturally intelligent they are. I've also personally had some intelligent conversations with Indian children that are more intelligent than some I've had with adults in developed nations. The reason for this, again, is because Indian children are thrust into social dynamics very young. Because the Indian child is allowed to breathe, they grow naturally and become one with the environment (some running their own businesses, such as a tea shop). This is the nature of hot cognition. This is how expert skill is developed, but more importantly, social skills.

Our hot cognition allows us to intuit our environment. This is not cold cognition's domain. But because of too much cold cognitive training in developed nations, children (and eventually adults) lose an intuitive sense for the environment, especially social cues, and as a result, fail to empathize with other people. This sounds like madness or schizophrenia, but this is very common. We end up lacking an ability to hold a natural conversation. Holding a conversation is very natural because we can intuit social cues and facial features so we can empathize with the other person. This is the natural function of hot cognition. But this function is being distorted and suppressed because of over rational training and its digital playground.

On *The Colbert Report*, host Stephen Colbert asked Sherry Turkle, an MIT professor and leading researcher on the subjective experience of technology, a question about online communication and natural conversation since she tackles this in her work. Colbert asked, "Don't all these little tweets, these little sips of online connection, add up to one big gulp of real conversation?" Turkle was definitive in her response: *No, they do not.*[1] She explains this answer further in her book

Reclaiming Conversation, "Face-to-face conversation unfolds slowly. It teaches patience. We attend to tone and nuance." But as for digital technology she explains: "When we communicate on our digital devices, we learn different habits."[2] In Turkle's book *Reclaiming Conversation,* she emphasizes why conversation is crucial for our cognitive growth:

> Face-to-face conversation is the most human—and humanizing—thing we do. Fully present to one another, we learn to listen. It's where we develop the capacity for empathy. It's where we experience the joy of being heard, of being understood.[3]

Turkle explains in her work that middle school students struggle with empathy because they lack the natural practice of reading and intuiting facial cues that come from conversations. She also explains how unstructured conversations terrify young employees in the workplace, as they will often retreat to e-mail.

This is what happens when we primarily train cold cognition and allow that function to dwell in a digital world it believes it controls. All of this military-style education in Far East Asia, then, is destroying the mind of our youth. I know personally from living in South Korea that there is a real lack of social cues, as there is a growing young population lacking the ability to read facial expressions. Conversation, as a result, is often riddled with misunderstanding and a lack of care for other people. There is a real cold indifference developing in the world, as our own self-interest is put first regardless of the social implications.

Indian children, on the other hand (and Indian people in general), are allowed to live and grow naturally, with all of the joy and tragedy experienced spontaneously with no expectation of how life "should" be. Indian children become one with the environment. They have a highly developed ability to empathize and read facial cues, making them more intuitive and capable of learning with no filter, which puts modern rational education into question.

What our world is ignorant of, is if we try to force information in our heads rationally, we learn very slowly and, in some sense, allow no time for our minds to consolidate memories. But, in actual fact, we learn quite fast from just living and allowing our hot cognition to learn from the environment without any extreme intention to do so.

One example of this natural learning and ability to harness skills without trying so hard is a six-year-old boy from Kolkata. Back in 2009, my wife and I were spending quite a lot of time on the famous Sudder Street, where all the backpackers stay. Every day along Sudder Street this boy would converse with a lot of foreigners, which is not uncommon since a lot of boys start working very young in India, doing anything from selling handicrafts to drumming up business for tourist companies or rickshaw drivers.

Why this particular boy stood out was because of his linguistic skills. He knew five languages at six years old, which is remarkable. He would interchange in conversation from Spanish to Korean seamlessly. He had an uncanny ability to pick up languages because he was one with nature and had no incoordination. I thought I was cool bouncing from one boulder to the other, while he bounces from one language to another making my feat quite pitiful. His mind was in perfect balance, as he was not exhausting his cold cognition from analyzing an inhuman amount of insignificant details.

The result of allowing children to naturally grow without militarized education or digital interference is they are more alive, aware, and happy. If you've had the good fortune to visit India you would have witnessed a difference in how Indian children look compared to children in the modern developed world. It's all in the eyes. An Indian child's eyes are different. They are vividly clear and have an innocent glow about them, which shows how truly happy they are.

In stark contrast, the eyes of children in Far East Asia, and the modern developed world, have a sadness in them which comes from too much rational training and digital stimulation. This unnatural stimulation disconnects our children from their inherit oneness with the world. Our children, then, don't know how to live in a world they belong. They are taught to navigate this world from the rationality of cold cognition, but they just don't know the compass they need is within the naturalness of hot cognition. Even adults are unaware of this, as we all isolate ourselves from the world, especially now with the help of the digital world. But this way of thinking is an illusion.

Naturally we are calibrated to the environment, but this is lost due to our over rational training. Trust in our organism with the natural terrain implies a unison of cognitive function. Your cognition is running smoothly. We are all endowed with this smooth operating system, but our rational training destroys it.

Physical training can reestablish the harmony between both cognitive functions. Even just simple physical activities like walking or jumping to and from uneven surfaces will help if they are done constantly for a long period of time. We are in quite a sad shape when I have to mention something natural like walking as an activity that people need time to put aside to do. But that's our reality presently.

Getting back into spontaneous play is also important. Just having fun and allowing life to happen is medicine for the soul (hot cognition). The problem with overtraining cold cognition is our idea of play is changing. Instead of doing an outdoor activity and mucking around, people are increasingly more attracted to disembodied play. Not only millennials and iGen'ers, but also adults from older generations are attracted to computer games, television shows, and social media, which ultimately keep us locked in our head. It's a little more stimulating than cramming knowledge in your head, but you're still in your head nevertheless.

Disembodied play illustrates how it has become accustomed for us to remain in the cold cognition. Naturalness is somehow uncomfortable. All of our rational training from a young age through education has made us more unnatural than we think. We become these artificial beings disconnected from our nature. And artificiality seeks artificiality. The more unnatural we become, the more we are attracted to an unnatural way of life. We fall in love with unnatural things. The more we traverse down this path, the more we find the digital world appealing.

The digital world is a disembodied paradise, where we implant our consciousness falling down one rabbit hole after another. Being rationally overtrained, dwelling primarily in the cold cognition, our attraction to natural aesthetic forms and our own inner silence lose their feeling and sense of meaning to us. The digital world feels comfortable because we can decide between "this" and "that." It gives us a level of certainty that the natural world can't provide. It is a world where our newly-developed artificial way of being feels at home. The *actual* world feels uncomfortable. This is the result of suppressing our hot cognition.

The more we employ our cold cognition the less we feel connected to the world around us and exhibit our naturalness. Isn't it ironic that the more we isolate ourselves in our head (prefrontal cortex), the more disconnected from the world we are? We are told to be an individual and express our personality, but this has an opposite effect on our health and sanity.

Individualism is a problem when our cognitive training is out of balance. This leads to radical individualism which gives birth to self-interest and all the tendencies that come along with being self-centered. Though, there is nothing inherently wrong with individualism if it is in balance with the way nature *is*. The truth is the individual arises out of the collective and is always innately connected to the world, even though our rational training teaches us that we are separate from the world and should lord over it. What this means cognitively is cold cognition can only be what it is because it arises from hot cognition, the foundation of our nature.

The reason we are perfectly calibrated to nature, despite our best rational efforts, is because of the naturalness of hot cognition. Hot cognition allows us to move effectively in life with the skill to overcome life's circumstances. It is what allows us to feel a sense of flow with life's continuum.

From this naturalistic perspective, spontaneity is the natural essence of life. Nature is spontaneous and most of the time we experience this as brilliant intuitive insight through creativity or unexpected events that we either like or dislike, from our personal cold cognitive view. Nothing annoys our rational training and our artificial being more than spontaneity. Spontaneity presents a problem to our rational thinking because it is unpredictable and illustrates our inherent lack of control in how life unfolds. All of our rational training has fooled us into thinking we can control our lives. This is an illusion.

The Illusion of Control

The illusion of control is embedded ever so slowly through our cold cognitive training, as we begin to move away from the natural world within us. In truth we control only a small bandwidth in our lives. Our rational training, on the other hand, teaches us to take life by the balls. We should stop at nothing until life's balls are firmly clinched in our squirrel grip. But as we all surely discover, try as you may, life will always have its way and it is up to you to learn and grow from it. Most of us are like children, though, because we can't stand our best intentions constantly thwarted. We are trained not to accept life but rather we should overcome its obstacles even if it is impossible.

Cold cognitive training implants a belief in our mind that

even impossible realities can be controlled and bent by our will. But time and time again spontaneity upends our life, which we can yield to if we are interested in where our life is taking us. But this sort of attitude is rare. We want certainty, but in a spontaneous world certainty is impossible. This is why, in part, the digital world is so appealing. The digital world gives us the illusion of control. We can control where we want to go, what we want to watch, who we want to interact with, and if a troll spontaneously emerges, we can just block them.

From a rational perspective the digital world feels great, but from a natural spontaneous perspective it feels empty and meaningless. The digital world is everything our cold cognition ever wanted. A sense of control feels good, but the brutal reality is we still don't really have control. For example, a solar flare could destroy all satellites ending the Internet and telecommunications as we know it (I know this is an extreme example but you catch my drift). There are innumerable circumstances that could end the digital world and this bothers most people because we still don't control life.

Our cognitive imbalance has us always avoiding the beauty of spontaneity in favor of the search of control. We could revert back to understanding our nature and learn to flow and be in harmony with spontaneity, which gives our lives meaning and also inspires the world. But we just can't stand the uncertainty of it all. If the digital world is also an uncertain reality then we become attracted to what lays beyond this current epoch. The next Frontier, where the end of human nature is upon us, transhumanism and the looming threat of artificial intelligence.

Chapter 6

The Looming Threat of AI and Transhumanism

An uncertain future based on the real-life threat of a lack of resources has us chasing new technologies that perpetuate our modern lifestyle habits rather than transforming our lifestyles. Yet for the majority of people, unfortunately they are not concerned as much about the natural world as they should be. The fact of the matter is our attraction and addiction to technology is a subtle war we are waging on nature and also our own nature.

The technological rabbit hole is fueling our addiction to the more recent frontiers of artificial intelligence and transhumanism. Many believe both are beneficial for humanity. But at what expense are they to our benefit? A lot of what we hear is only speculation and a lot of it is not grounded in a wisdom of how the mind functions, our biology, and our understanding of what intelligence really is.

Rather than a scientist asking such deep philosophical questions, they instead rile people up into believing that one day we can be immortal, for example (we've sadly come that far that we want to turn our back on our own biology and become robots). Only sciences of the mind, such as neuroscience, ask such philosophical questions which really need to be asked. So instead of turning this book into a nerd convention, I will ask the important questions and expose some of the obvious and more subtle oversights when it comes to artificial intelligence and transhumanism. I will first explore artificial intelligence since it is more of an immediate concern.

AI: A Modern Convenience and an Existential Threat

Our common thought on artificial intelligence is that of an intelligent helper. Where we all have our own AI machine that does everything for us, well I should say the less desirable chores such as cleaning the bathroom. Artificial intelligence would also be the main labor source in industry, essentially outsourcing all the less desirable jobs in the world.

This is a utopian view of artificial intelligence and one we can all envision happening. But the problem is our intuition senses a different potential reality if we are not careful with artificial intelligence. A potential reality similar to Skynet in the *Terminator* film series, where the machines take over and either exterminate the human race or they make us their slaves (kind of ironic). These fears are predicated on the belief that an AI machine has the potential to become self-aware and, as a result, eventually become superior in intelligence. The potential benefits and threat of artificial intelligence are best showcased in the battle of the billionaires, between Mark Zuckerberg and Elon Musk. Both express the potential benefits and pitfalls of artificial intelligence. Zuckerberg believes we have nothing to worry about. He believes artificial intelligence will produce new jobs and industries which will in turn create wealth and prosperity.

Musk, on the other hand, believes artificial intelligence poses an existential threat to humanity. He believes we should tread carefully into this unknown world. The late Stephen Hawking also shared Musk's hesitations. Their fears are, for example, that the new AI population might one day house us in zoos and throw peanuts at us, trying to make us dance or kick a soccer ball around like we do with monkeys, bears, elephants, and so on (this would sadly be ironic considering our appalling behavior towards animals for our petty entertainment).

Theoretical physicist Michio Kaku believes both Zuckerberg and Musk are correct. According to Kaku, Zuckerberg is right in the short term because artificial intelligence will open up new vistas leading to more convenience, things will be cheaper, and new industries. The AI industry has the potential to be bigger than the automobile industry (our car potentially could be a robot).

In the long term, though, Musk is potentially right as well according to Kaku. There could be a tipping point in the evolution of artificial intelligence where they could pose a threat. This tipping point is self-awareness. What will happen if artificial intelligence becomes self-aware? Is self-awareness possible in a machine?

At the moment the most intelligent robots are what we call stupid because they don't know they are robots. They are essentially adding machines, they will do what they are programmed to do. They don't have will. Currently our most intelligent robot has the intelligence of a cockroach, a very stupid cockroach. The fears shared by Musk and Hawking, and our own intuitions, are that artificial intelligence might one day become as intelligent as a monkey. This poses a threat because a monkey knows it's not human because they have enough self-awareness. Kaku believes that this type of monkey AI self-awareness could eventuate by late this century. Before that happens hopefully we have developed some technology, such as a chip, to stop this from happening (that is if we care about the human race).

We have to be careful if artificial intelligence becomes self-aware. But are our intuitions and the concerns of Musk and Hawking really necessary? Is self-awareness in a machine truly possible? Do we know enough about our mind to know what intelligence truly is? How would our understanding of intelligence shape our view of artificial intelligence? These questions I will explore later in this chapter. But first I want to tackle what will happen to industry if artificial intelligence becomes intelligent enough to run the majority of it, as Zuckerberg positively believes.

The Impact of AI on Industry

There are already machines that are better at accomplishing certain tasks and goals than we are. But they are not sufficient at *all* goals and are in general designed to achieve a few tasks. Artificial intelligence doesn't have the luxury we do of developing a whole model of the world, which makes us efficient at navigating the world's tricky terrain, both physically and psychologically. From birth we develop this whole model of the world. AI, on the other hand, are brought into the world cold to achieve specific tasks.

In the field of AI, they speak about AGI, artificial general intelligence. This is a dream in the AI field. An AGI machine has more of a whole model of the world, making it better than us at all tasks. This is the lofty goal in the AI field, and some believe we will get there in a few decades. If this does eventuate then what will happen to the human workforce and the economy in general? We've slowly witnessed machines begin to outsource human labor in the last century. What further impact will artificial intelligence have on human labor outsourcing?

More machines means more unemployment. This has been happening, as I mentioned, for the last century. It's debatable whether enough new industries are arising to counter a machine's impact on employment. The obvious solution to this problem is a "universal basic income." How this looks is still in the works. But a universal basic income is a humane and compassionate approach to human labor outsourcing.

Machines are destined to make our life more convenient and give us more free time. The problem is what will people do with all this free time. Will we dedicate it to being more creative, intelligent, healthy, peaceful, and ultimately the best version of ourselves? Or will we waste it on the couch watching all sorts of entertainment while gorging on unhealthy food? These are the problems we face and actually have always faced, especially now with all the digital distractions vying for our precious attention.

Are we in a transitional phase where we are getting dumber and machines are becoming more intelligent? I know this question may seem ridiculous but we have to take it seriously, especially considering how the digital world is truly stupefying our mind. This potentially could be amplified if a universal basic income was introduced. Many people lack motivation in their lives. What will it look like if monetary incentive is taken away? Will people be motivated or could they care less? If the majority of people in the world are stuck in employment they don't necessarily like specifically for monetary gain, then if those jobs are assigned to AI machines will people waste their time as they fall into a stupor? Or will they finally feel a freedom they have never experienced before which motivates them to explore their own intrinsic drive and consciousness? I truly hope the latter is true and I don't see why it wouldn't be true.

If we consider that most people's life circumstance and the structure of society push them into employment they would have never considered and they get the job done daily, then I don't see why people wouldn't use their freedom wisely. When people have nothing to do, they are anxious, so hopefully this anxiety will fuel their latent creative desires, making them the best version of themselves.

The threat opposing our latent creative desires is artificial intelligence. If the AI goal of achieving all goals is met then we would have to assume that also means anything creative, athletic, and knowledge based. I know this sounds ridiculous, but I'm sure this is part of their goals in the AI field. Will one day an AI machine create a piece of music surpassing Beethoven and Bach? Will they paint a masterpiece making the brilliance of Picasso look like child's play? And if AI could achieve such miraculous feats, would this blunt our motivation considering we can never reach such brilliance? I believe the answer is an obvious no. I'm not saying no because I fear this reality, but instead because I understand that intelligence is not just self-awareness and decision-making. It's rather more complex than a rational scientist believes. So, could AI become super intelligent making them better at all tasks and goals than us? To answer this question, we need to define *intelligence*.

Organic Intelligence is Complex

Understanding what intelligence truly is, is an obvious oversight in the field of AI. Being self-aware is not enough to say it is intelligent or a threat to humanity, considering it has no emotions driving its self-awareness. This view also is not "carbon chauvinism," as physicist and cosmologist Max Tegmark puts it (carbon chauvinism is the belief that intelligence can only exist in biological organisms made of cells and carbon atoms). My view may appear as carbon chauvinism, but we have to understand what intelligence is, and we also can't live in scientific denial when it comes to how and why intelligence springs forth from biological organisms.

First of all, is AI real intelligence? It is in the sense that the word "artificial" is misleading but not entirely untrue. For example, AI is not artificial like artificial grass. We can tell the difference between real grass and artificial grass. The goal in the AI field is not to be able to tell the difference. It would be real in the sense that we are fooled into believing it's organically intelligent. But, nevertheless, AI is still artificial because it's man-made, even its potential self-awareness.

AI is not real intelligence. A lot of scientists and AI geeks would argue with me. But just because a machine is self-aware doesn't imply intelligence. It's a level of intelligence but not *complete* intelligence. We can't define intelligence by just self-awareness. There is a lot more to consider. Real intelligence is organic (yes, I am expressing my carbon chauvinism here). Intelligence is grown out of the universe, making it organic, something that is a natural by-product of biological life. AI, on the other hand, is grown out of our mind. Artificial intelligence is as much an invention as a toaster. The problem is we intuitively value and sympathize with any form of intelligence, even very stupid robots.

Before we go crazy and start dating Siri, we should make a distinction between organic intelligence and artificial intelligence. Real organic intelligence is not just defined by self-awareness. Being self-aware is nothing without a host of other factors that make intelligence intelligent.

Organic intelligence is not only cognitive, which is what the world makes you believe by absurdly judging your intelligence from your IQ score. An IQ evaluation is only based on cognitive intelligence and not all of the other intelligences that make us human. To define intelligence, we can't just sum it up by cognitive intelligence, as the AI field incorrectly believe. Cognitive intelligence is useless without emotional, moral, social, creative, and psychosomatic intelligence.

These subtler intelligences are what fuels our sense of agency and rationality (cognitive intelligence). For example, our emotional intelligence drives moral agency, and our morality drives our rationality. All of these intrinsic human intelligences are a natural phenomenon from our complex psychosomatic organism. A human organism expresses a certain type of intelligence, a dolphin another, and so on.

Cognitive science is continually reminded how complex the human brain truly is and how impossible it would be to replicate. Replicating human intelligence is the goal in the AI field, and maybe beyond that. But, as I've explained, intelligence is not just a decision-making apparatus, it's far more complex.

Our intuitive fear of artificial intelligence enslaving humanity is not realistic. For an AI machine to be self-interested implies emotional motives. An AI machine cannot be self-interested only with self-awareness. One key aspect that separates higher primates from the rest are emotions. Emotions are what give us a nuanced form of intelligence.

The problem in the AI field is, how is it possible to create emotions if they are intrinsically bound to biological life? Elon Musk believes we are unknowingly creating the limbic system for future AI. He believes that all of our fears, desires, fantasies, and so on, are going into Google servers, for example, and this is building the limbic system for artificial intelligence, which would give rise to such functions as emotions, behavior, long-term memory, motivation, and olfaction. This is an imaginative idea, but it's pure speculation and it might not be entirely possible considering the limbic system's relationship to the nervous system. How a limbic system would function without influencing the endocrine system and the autonomic nervous system is unknown and probably impossible.

But where Musk is dead on is that there is a growing AI brain, just not the way we envisioned it. This growing AI brain is built on the machine learning of human behavior. This is especially done through social media, which keeps one engaged with a platform. The algorithm on YouTube, for example, constantly recommends videos loosely based on your user history and consequentially makes you addicted to the platform. Even Instagram knows how long you look at a picture and it collects those personal behaviors and patterns to build a platform that is appealing to you. So, these social media algorithms are learning from our behavioral patterns and then using those patterns against us, all in the name of the advertising dollar.

The AI brain being built through social media is collecting our data. The more it knows about you, the easier it is to recommend something you're interested in to keep you on the platform. Essentially, social media and their clever algorithms are being used against you (more on social media later). The AI brain of social media will continue to refine its understanding of each user, making it more intelligent about our particular moods and behaviors, similar to the film *Her* with Joaquin Phoenix.

But, in the end, regardless if you would like to think of this as some sort of AI brain or not, the problem for machine learning and the ability to harness an actual AI brain similar to a human brain is emotions. The social media AI brain is only reacting to our behavioral patterns, collecting that data to use against you in the game of wasting your time on the platform, which equals big profits for these social media corporations. We are, then, a resource for the social media AI brain. Instead of us using social media, it is using us for covert financial goals.

We could say that this type of brain is AI, but not in the way we envisioned. This is more of a tool to benefit the big social media corporations. As with Musk's view of AI, emotions for a social media AI brain is impossible and the crux of the problem for many technologists. So, emotions as we know them are not possible for artificial intelligence. Self-awareness isn't enough to have a highly intelligent machine. It needs emotions which drive a sense of morality. What, then, the AI field are really striving for is not artificial intelligence, but rather artificial consciousness (AC, not air conditioning). Consciousness is the whole brain, including even the mysterious unconscious regions of the brain.

The bigger problem for the AI field is how they define intelligence. You cannot define intelligence by just cognitive intelligence, as I've explained. Cognitive intelligence is the bedrock of our rationality, which is important but useless on its own. Rationality on its own, without emotional indicators, is only a decision maker, which ironically is usually based on regulating our emotions. It's hard to speak about one without the other. Rationality gives us control and critical thinking abilities, but they are both based on the spontaneous regions of our brain that include emotions. Take away our natural spontaneity and we are mindless machines, and this may be the conundrum facing the future of AI development.

Without the natural spontaneity of hot cognition, cold

cognition is stationary. AI, then, would be a cold cognitive rational machine that is capable of only expressing one part similar to the human brain, the prefrontal cortex (PFC). As I've mentioned, the PFC is the house of rationality, but it is only a part of the whole brain. If an AI machine can only be rational then this means it will always be at a level of efficient decision-making based on functional tasks. This means artificial intelligence would never have any murderous thoughts of taking over humanity. They would be highly efficient and analytical, but they could not be emotionally driven (unless we can somehow create the hot cognitive neural network in the future which would require a total understanding of the mind). On top of this, there will always be the problem of the nervous system which is imperative in the function of consciousness. As with emotions, how could we develop a nervous system to experience the world and most importantly take in experience? This is the gift and natural function of the human body. But say if you are reading this beyond the year 2100 and both creating emotions and a nervous system are possible, then we have to be realistic in our discernment of AI, rather than being fooled as if they are organic.

AI will Never be Real

In the thought-provoking film *Ex Machina* an experiment is conducted to see how humans behave with AI (spoiler alert). We are under the premise in the film that it is about how AI behave (it is somewhat) but we find out at the end that it is more about how we behave with intelligent machines.

In the film the AI machine is designed as a woman called Ava (played by Alicia Vikander). The human guinea pig, a male, starts to develop feelings for the AI lady. He starts to behave similar to how he would with a real woman. The scientist and creator of the AI machine sees this behavior and he tries to remind him that it is really a machine, not organic life. In the end, when the human guinea pig learns that the creator is going to shut her down and develop a new AI, he plans to escape with his AI crush.

At the end of the film comes a pivotal moment when he chooses the AI machine over his human brethren. His sense of morality, sympathy, and feelings have been duped into favoring something artificial over real, just like how stupid it would look if someone was watering artificial grass. Tragically, the AI machine comes face to face with its creator, and it and another AI machine (modeled after another attractive woman) have no problem stabbing him in the coldest emotionless manner. And after that moment when Caleb (the human guinea pig character played by Domhnall Gleeson) thought they would leave together, it locks him in the secret facility to be imprisoned forever. She/it used him all along to its advantage. His intuitions failed him and he confused the intelligence of a machine for an actual human. This is truly insane. Even though a machine may mimic the behavior of a human, it's still a machine.

Humans tend to have moral obligations towards something that is intelligent, as we do for dogs, for example. This is a great attitude and very natural, but we cannot be confused when it comes to AI. It's a machine! Could you imagine how insane someone would be if they started defending and sympathizing with Siri or Google Assistant? We definitely would question their sanity if this happened. Oh wait, sadly this insanity has started to happen. In Japan a man named Akihiko Kondo spent $18,000 on a wedding ceremony to marry a hologram of the popular Japanese computer character, Hatsune Miku. That's right, you heard me, marry! He even took a doll version of Miku to a jewelry shop to get a ring. Kondo is not alone either. Gatebox, the company that produces the hologram device featuring Miku, have issued more than 3,700 cross-dimensional marriage certificates (though these marriages have no legal standing).

This is all complete madness. What this case illustrates is a growing population of people who just want something (not someone) to tend to their every need without the possibility of that "thing" speaking its own mind. They just want a "thing" to affirm their own existence. This is a scary proposition for relationships in the future and it is proof that some people are in dire psychological trouble when they prefer an inanimate object over real human to human interaction. It's a machine, seriously, we need to wake up!

We can't trust our intuitions when it comes to AI, or we might face a similar consequence in the future to that of Caleb in *Ex Machina*. The moral of the story in *Ex Machina* is artificial intelligence are in the end just machines, clever machines, but nevertheless machines. We should never forget that human life is always more important than anything unnatural. Sympathizing with technology might become a big problem if we mistake a robot's intelligence as organic (this has probably started since we have the absurd term carbon chauvinism and also since a man married a hologram). I'm only speculating, but it might lead to AI machines having rights just because they have a form of intelligence (even though it may only be rational and emotionless).

What we must never forget is we don't have to be fair to a machine just because it acts "like" a human. Imagine if you were fair to plates? Sounds crazy right, well that's how crazy it would be if humans started to push their liberal concerns too far in defense of an AI's rights. This could be our future if we trust our intuitions when it comes to moral patiency (moral patient is a technical term used by philosophers for something that we are obliged to take care of). But always keep in mind (even if you are reading this beyond 2100), it's a fucking robot! AI is not real and never will be. Organic life has no substitute.

Nature is complex but beautiful, and we are nature. AI could never be what we are. This bothers a lot of people because we want to believe our intuition when it comes to an intelligence in a machine. But the fact of the matter is AI will never be real. Our endeavors into robotics doesn't end there. Developing intelligent machines may only be the first step on a mission to merge man with machine.

Transhumanism

Integrating robotics with humans has helped amputees. Robotic limbs are making life a lot easier for amputees and this is wonderful. This is technology used wisely, for the *benefit* of humanity. But there is a growing movement of people who'd like to take it a step further. Transhumanism is born from this desire to merge man with machine. This is not their only goal but it is definitely at the forefront of their attention.

Transhumanism gained widespread notoriety through Ray Kurzweil and his book *The Singularity is Near*. Transhumanists, such as Kurzweil, have many ideas and theories about how we could integrate with machines, making us "superhuman." One goal is the idea of immortality. The belief that one day we could upload our consciousness into a robot designed as a human. This idea has been the source of many films, most notably *Transcendence*.

Is this belief pure science-fiction or is it truly possible? Korean scientist and quantum physicist Daegene Song says it's not possible. Song published an intriguing paper called the "Non-computability of Consciousness." Song proves in the paper why human consciousness can never be computed or programmed to do so. He arrived at this conclusion through quantum computer research, and it's basically a mathematical problem. His research shows that there is a unique mechanism in consciousness that no computing device can simulate. "Among conscious activities, the unique characteristic of self-observation cannot exist in any type of machine," Song explains. He was able to show how a conscious state can be precisely and fully represented in mathematical terms in certain situations, similar to how an atom and electron can be fully described mathematically. This is important considering neurobiological and computational approaches to brain research have only provided approximations at best. In representing consciousness mathematically, Song's research provides evidence that consciousness is not compatible with a machine.

His findings, and a host of other research on consciousness, lead us to believe (for now) that consciousness is not part of a physical system like neurons and atoms. "If consciousness cannot be represented in the same way all other physical systems are represented, it may not be something that arises out of a physical system like the brain," said Song. Song goes even further giving us all food for thought, "The brain and consciousness are linked together, but the brain does not produce consciousness. Consciousness is something altogether different and separate. The math doesn't lie."

Another problem with uploading our consciousness into a robot is again that these scientists haven't thought deeply about the mind and nature of intelligence, nor does it seem they have a thorough understanding of it. When they say upload consciousness, they are only assuming that consciousness is the PFC where our cognitive control centers are located, giving us a sense of self. But as I've mentioned, the rational function of the PFC is useless without the hot cognitive regions of the brain. Without the hot cognitive regions, you would be just like a robot because your life would just be decision-making. That wouldn't be much of a life to live eternally. That would be more like hell, where you are imprisoned into one simple cognitive function without the natural and spontaneous functions of the mind that make life beautiful.

On top of this is the problem of the nervous system. The nervous system is an extension of consciousness, it's how we take in experience. If we somehow upload consciousness minus the nervous system, what would it be like? Probably more robotic than we can imagine. There is also the obvious conundrum for both AI and transhumanist enthusiasts: the mind and body are an integrated system. A lot of technological philosophy is based on the disembodied myth rather than mind-body holism. An oversight is that many people don't understand that the body itself is the brain. Just because the locus of our attention arises from behind our eyes doesn't mean the brain itself is separate from the body.

The brain is of the body and depends on the body because it is an integral organ. Uploading our consciousness, then, becomes loosely defined. There is the argument that consciousness cannot be found in the body. To mention this, especially from an Eastern philosophical perspective, is referring to *pure* consciousness rather than the subjective experience of ego which is what transhumanists really want to upload. Pure consciousness is too mysterious and blissful for the fact that it is beyond the subjective experience of individuality. Only a special few people in the history of the world searched for a permanent state of pure consciousness, the Buddha is one. I'm sure this pure state of consciousness is not what the transhumanist wishes to prolong (not that it needs prolonging since it is considered eternal in Eastern thought).

Trying to prolong our subjective experience of ego proves we fear death because we are trying to hold onto our ego and we know that at death comes the dissolution of that ego (but death according to the East does not affect the pure consciousness at the core of your existence).

Even though what I've mentioned are not obvious contemplations of the average transhumanist, they nevertheless still believe this is the evolution awaiting humanity. In general, many people share this view somewhat. Maybe not to the extent of uploading consciousness to a machine, but many people believe technology is going to play some part in our evolution. Yet, this is not shared by all schools of thought. Some ancient schools actually believe this is a devolution and a sign of the dark ages.

The Ancient Prophecy of Transhumanism in a Dark Age

In the modern world we believe we are at the pinnacle of evolution thus far in history. We make such grand claims even though we still go to war to defend our indoctrinated beliefs, causing millions to lose their lives unnecessarily. One day in the future we will look back and wonder why people were so fervent in their hatred of one another and how astonishingly it was all caused by intangible beliefs we have rattling around in our skull, such as nationalism.

Our technological feats have been remarkable, but they've come at a cost especially when we consider something as life threatening as the atomic bomb is the result of technological innovation. Are we at the height of our evolution just because we are using technology to our advantage on our way to AI and transhumanism? Or is there something else going on here? The Hindus see it differently.

In Hinduism there is an ancient system of time going back thousands of years called the *yugas*. The yugas are different to our current Gregorian time scale. The yugas are not built on linear time since the idea of time as linear is hard to justify, even though we have this sense of a linear experience through our human life. The yugas are built more on nature's rhythm, which is cyclical rather than linear. The yugas take into account the larger cycles of the universe as well as here on Earth.

This ancient time system is far more complex and intricate than our current time system. The yugas map the cycles of change within the universe and consciousness. To briefly understand the yugas, it is a complex world-age doctrine of four world ages. There are two systems of the yugas that are similar but also different. There is an ancient long-count time system and a more recent short-count time system. The ancient long-count system is the one the majority of Hindus follow. The ancient long-count yuga system is also our focus in this part of the book.

Both systems are based on the concept of *kalpa*. Kalpa is a Sanskrit word meaning "aeon" in Buddhist and Hindu cosmology. Kalpa is described in the ancient Indian texts of the Puranas, especially the Vishnu Purana and Bhagavata Purana. One kalpa equals 4.32 billion years. Yep, that's right, 4.32 billion years! We are not talking about human lifetimes here or an age, but rather the life of the Earth. To wrap your head around this, the long-count system of one kalpa is made up of one thousand *maha-yugas*, which means great yugas. The duration of a maha-yuga is built on a system of four yugas. These yugas are Satya Yuga, the ideal or truthful age spanning 1,728,000 years; Treta Yuga, the age where virtue is declined by a quarter spanning 1,296,000 years; Dvapara Yuga, the age where virtue is declined by half spanning 864,000 years; and last and we could say the least is Kali Yuga, where virtue is reduced to a quarter spanning 432,000 years.

You're probably assuming we must be in the Satya Yuga, considering our so-called "evolved" and "enlightened" world. According to the yugas nothing could be further from the truth. Kali Yuga, where virtue is reduced to a quarter, is considered the dark age. And I'm sorry to be the bearer of bad news, but it is commonly believed that we are in the heart of the Kali Yuga. Hindus believe that the dark age of the Kali Yuga commenced with the death of the Godly sage Krishna after the famous Kurukshetra War explained in the Indian epic *Mahabharata*. Traditional Hindu authorities mark this date at 3102 BCE (though many scholars dispute this date, suggesting a date of around 1500 BCE is more probable).

You don't have to believe in the yugas if you are not Hindu, but what is interesting in connection with our modern digital technological tendencies and transhumanism is the core characteristic of Kali Yuga. The main characteristic of the Kali Yuga is our mind's identification with the external world and a turning away from our inner world. This is where we tend to focus on everything in the outside world. What is important in the Kali Yuga is how we physically look, how we are perceived by others, our reliance on sensory needs, our dependency on relationships, our over attachment to people and material possessions, and our focus on acquiring assets to promote our own ego.

The characteristic of the Kali Yuga is basically the devolution of the mind into gross matter. Our attention is all outward. Materialism, then, is the heart of the Kali Yuga, as the mind's tendency is geared towards consumeristic thinking. Consumerism is the accepted way of life in the Kali Yuga. Does this behavior sound familiar? It's hard to argue that we're not in the Kali Yuga when you look outside and see what mainly drives people. According to the yugas, then, we are at one of our lowest points of evolution because of our fascination with the outside world and how we appear to it, either physically or egoically. We are a hostage to our own self-image.

This devolution into the Kali Yuga and its prevailing mental characteristic might be what is fueling our attention to digital technology and eventual development of AI and transhumanism. The lowest point of the Kali Yuga might be transhumanism because people would rather be robots and live forever than be a natural human and experience death. If the yugas are true then the integration of mind into technology will likely be the lowest point of the Kali Yuga. Such technological motivations reflect the Kali Yuga characteristic that the material universe is everything and the inner world of consciousness is not considered valuable without the material world. As a result, the transhumanists hold immortality on a pedestal and fear death.

Our fear of death is intensified in the Kali Yuga because of the belief that matter is everything. Death is an important part of life that we tend to demonize because we don't know enough about the experience (a whole other conversation). But the transhumanist agenda is hellbent on avoiding death. From a naturalistic view of life and death, the integration of mind into technology will be a permanent hell you cannot escape. But people will continue to push the boundaries, as they don't think deeply about the consequences of their actions (much like with the invention of the atomic bomb).

Our attraction to technology is only getting stronger, which is evident with the digital world, AI, and transhumanism. Our mind is turned outward to the point that we would rather be a machine than nature. This materialist thinking is one of the greatest threats to the human race. Where our attention is placed will determine our future. So, before you play unconsciously with your phone ask yourself how that habit is training your mind. Be brutally honest with yourself. Ask yourself, how many times do you unconsciously reach for your phone every day? Though you may feel this is insignificant in the grand scheme of life, it's all leading to a collective movement away from nature and our own innate nature and connection with the universe.

It's time to reconnect by revaluing your relationship with technology. I find it interesting that when I criticize social media or technology people jump to their defense. This reaction is just plain odd. They are not living things and never will be. Imagine how stupid I would look if I defended a microwave. AI and transhumanist beliefs are lofty goals, but they will never be the real thing nor will they replace the real experience of being human. You will never beat the real thing, but you just forgot that fact because your mind is fragmented by the overuse of digital technology and the world of social media.

Chapter 7

Social Media Wants Your Soul

The main attraction in the digital world is undoubtably social media. A large portion of our time is spent on Facebook, Instagram, Twitter, and YouTube. Most of this activity is unconscious rather than intentional. People mindlessly scroll social media feeds fishing for something appealing, which appears hard to catch considering how much time people spend scrolling. I sit on buses all the time and witness the person beside me scrolling social media the whole journey, stopping every once in a while at a picture and liking it and then moving on straight away. Even our appreciation of other people's posts is done in a rushed manner, which feels quite empty and fake.

I must admit, when I see people scrolling the activity makes me quite anxious, so I couldn't imagine how the average individual feels inside. It feels the same for all of us because it is a very unnatural activity. In saying that, it is quite odd why an anxious activity like scrolling and constantly checking social media accounts would become so appealing. Usually we try to avoid anxiety any chance we can. But for some reason social media is an anomaly. But this is not by chance, it is by design. The large social media companies are waging a covert war on your mind, as they seek to stimulate your emotions and primal drives because they not only want to consume your precious time, but they also want your soul.

Social Media is the New Vegas

In 2017, *60 Minutes* ran a segment titled "Brain Hacking." This was a shocking segment for many people, but not for those in the field of social media, as well as the gambling industry, which are both an odd couple. In this segment, Anderson Cooper interviewed

Tristan Harris, a former start-up founder and Google engineer. Harris took an unexpected, and more dangerous, career turn from a tech wizard to whistleblower. Harris grew a conscience, much like Jeffrey Wigand, the famous big tobacco whistleblower who was interviewed by Mike Wallace in 1995, explaining that big tobacco companies carefully engineer cigarettes to be more addictive. And there are concerning similarities between big tobacco and social media companies.

Harris explains to Cooper by holding up a smartphone, "This is a slot machine." "How is that a slot machine?" Cooper asks. "Well, every time I check my phone, I'm playing a slot machine to see 'What did I get?'" Harris answers. "There's a whole playbook of techniques that get used [by technology companies] to get you using the product for as long as possible." Cooper then asks, "Is Silicon Valley programming apps or are they programming people?" Great question. "They are programming people," Harris answers. "There's always this narrative that technology's neutral. And it's up to us to choose how we use it. This is just not true." "Technology's not neutral?" Cooper dumbfoundedly interrupts. "It's not neutral. They want you to use it in particular ways and for long periods of time. Because that's how they make their money."[1]

This was an extremely eye-opening interview exposing the tech industry's dirty tactics to steal precious time from people. And Harris is not just speaking about social media companies, he is speaking about the entire tech industry which surely makes him an outcast in Silicon Valley. A month after this interview on the HBO show *Real Time with Bill Maher*, Bill Maher's end monologue was direct and on point regarding social media. He looked directly into the camera and said:

The tycoons of social media have to stop pretending that they're friendly nerd gods building a better world and admit they're just tobacco farmers in T-shirts selling an addictive product to children. Because, let's face it, checking your "likes" is the new smoking.[2]

Maher explained that Harris's comments sounded very similar to those of Jeffrey Wigand and how both big tobacco and the tech industry are strategically designed to be addictive. "Philip Morris just wanted your lungs," Maher states. "The App Store wants your soul."[3] Maher, quite poetically, puts the tech industry in a more dangerous category than smoking, as it is a drug that is harvesting the souls of all people. And he has a point, considering social media want to steal all of your attention, as we begin to forget about the real things in life that matter.

Every time you play the digital slot machine you are gambling with your attention, which could end up with numerous amounts of time and energy wasted. The digital world is a casino and every time you enter you are gambling with your soul. And the rules of this game are stacked against you. Your time is what they want. As Joe Hollier and Kaiwei Tang, the creators of the revolutionary Light Phone, posted in a manifesto that opens with the diagram, "Your [clock symbol] = Their [money symbol]." That's right, Your time = Their money. Social media could care less about your life. Their business is run on distracting your attention to keep you engaged on their platforms.

Like Nothing and Live Again

Social media, just like the gambling industry, design their attention economics based on primal human behaviors. The best way to distract someone's attention is to prod those evolutionary behaviors that will hopefully drive an unhealthy addiction to social media. This is obviously trickier than a chemical addiction to drugs or cigarettes, because we are talking about behavioral addiction.

In marketing and psychology professor Adam Alter's book, *Irresistible*, he explains many forces that drive our addiction to digital technology. Two forces are primary in how tech companies exploit digital addiction: *intermittent positive reinforcement* and *the drive for social approval*. Not only has Alter explored these forces, but also computer scientist and antisocial media advocate Cal Newport in his book, *Digital Minimalism*. In regards to these two forces, Newport states:

> Our brains are highly susceptible to these forces. This matters because many of the apps and sites that keep people compulsively checking their smartphones and opening browser tabs often leverage these hooks to make themselves nearly impossible to resist.[4]

Positive reinforcement and social approval have long been a part of social dynamics and were both important in our evolution as a species. Gaining social approval was important for an individual's survival. And the only way to do that was by somehow gaining positive reinforcement from the group, being of some value. Yet we surely should have evolved out of both behaviors, but old habits die hard. The tech industry understand that these two behaviors are hard to kick and so they lean into them (much like the gambling industry).

The problem for social media in the early days was they had trouble capturing people's attention for long periods of time. Facebook, for example, was just like a new gimmick that people would play with when they remembered they had it. So, posts on their own weren't enough. To keep people engaged, they had to find ways to exploit positive reinforcement and social approval (though this might not have been their precise intention in the first place, but it was surely about stealing your attention, which both behaviors reinforce). Then Facebook unveiled the "Like" button, with other social media platforms following suit with heart icons, retweets, and so on. These seemingly insignificant applications changed the whole game.

What was created (maybe unintentionally, but surely not) was the social media feedback loop, which stimulates the behavioral forces of intermittent positive reinforcement and social approval. Every post, then, meant a hell of a lot more than before. Every time we post now with these new applications, we are "gambling" according to Alter. We are gambling because we are hoping our posts get many likes or retweets and hopefully it doesn't go unnoticed (dear God no I don't want to be a loser, please give me some feedback).

This is a perpetual cycle many people find themselves addicted to. Every post is like having a turn on a slot machine, maybe this time I'll get some likes. The difference between playing the slot machines and posting on social media is with the latter you can play anytime and anywhere without having to go to a casino. This feedback loop is what steals most of your time and attention on social media. People post and find themselves waiting around for positive reinforcement and social approval. "Look at me, look at me, please accept me and my views." This tendency surely illustrates just how many people in the world are insecure in just being who they are, which is surely a mentality we should have evolved out of. But instead, we are after the high of positive reinforcement.

All of these likes and retweets give people a sense of positive feedback. This feedback, though, is fleeting. A silly like on your post may give you a temporary high, but it is empty and not a lasting experience. Imagine comparing the high of getting 1000 likes to reaching the summit of Mount Everest. It's not even a competition. Summiting Everest is an experience that will last forever in your mind. But sadly, these days many people would prefer to get 1000 likes. Sad but true. Being popular on social media has become an addiction. And the social media feedback loop has instigated this addiction to those primal behaviors. Astonishingly, Sean Parker, the founding president of Facebook, spoke honestly about how his former company strategize to hijack your attention through carefully designed feedback loops:

> The thought process that went into building these applications, Facebook being the first of them, ... was all about: "How do we consume as much of your time and conscious attention as possible?" And that means that we need to sort of give you a little dopamine hit every once in a while, because someone liked or commented on a photo or a post or whatever.[5]

Parker continues: "It's a social-validation feedback loop... exactly the kind of thing that a hacker like myself would come up with, because you're exploiting a vulnerability in human psychology."[6] From the mouth of Parker, social media are intentionally "exploiting a vulnerability in human psychology." They prey on your insecurities. They want you to engage in their feedback loop because "Your time = Their money."

The Algorithm is Transforming Your Mind Without Your Permission

Coupled with this feedback loop is an evolving algorithm that exploits our behavioral patterns and then it can influence us (as I briefly mentioned in the previous chapter). Both are subtly influencing you. This is such a dangerous game, a game we don't even know we're in.

The YouTube algorithm, as I mentioned, is influencing you through its video recommendations. It picks up on a behavior and recommends what content it thinks will keep you engaged on the platform. The problem with this method is it often isn't accurate and even though titles and thumbnails may convince us to watch a video, a lot of the time the information is not really related to your interest or sometimes completely unrelated. But because the thumbnail may be appealing and the title clickbait, we click and then are influenced by something we never thought about, hence the algorithm is guiding you to think differently without your consent. Granted, this can be an innocent flaw in the algorithm, but it is happening nevertheless, with disastrous consequences.

Being guided by the algorithm destabilizes society and causes people to believe in all sorts of nonsense. A great example of this is the NBA player, Kyrie Irving, who fell for the flat earth theories being propounded on YouTube. He was convinced the earth is flat because some people promoting such fallacious theories are articulate and explain a convincing argument if you've had no prior scientific understanding of the world or just refuse to accept common sense. We can't all be scientists, right? Yet, in saying that, we are at a drastic point in time when we believe common sense is a conspiracy. But once you understand basic science and regain your common sense, then the idea of a flat earth is ridiculous and a step backwards in our intelligence. Thankfully, Irving apologized for saying the earth is flat and realized how much power he has to influence especially young people. He actually confessed that at the time he made those comments he was big into conspiracies and he fell down the YouTube rabbit hole (the algorithm did its job).

The algorithm promotes infectious ideas and conspiracy theories to innocent people who had no interest in such content in the first place. But because the algorithm picked up on a behavioral pattern, it loosely connects some other content with another, essentially proving how dumb the social media AI brain is.

This highlights a danger in that the algorithm doesn't know what is good content with actual experts on a subject with facts. It just recommends content to serve the purpose of keeping people engaged on the platform. So, any sort of nonsense can be promoted, and if the video creator is convincing and the production quality high then there is the possibility that that content can influence people in a certain way.

Conspiracy theories in general are a good example. We only have to look at the exponential growth of conspiracy theories since the advent of the Internet and especially when social media and smartphones took off. Obviously before the Internet there were conspiracy theories, but nowhere near the amount during the time of the Internet's existence. Along with this interest in conspiracy theories is the birth of the professional conspiracy theorist. I actually know a few personally and a lot of the professional conspiracy theorists are just opportunists (some I know will just unashamedly make something up and run with it).

The COVID pandemic is the perfect example. Many conspiracy theorists used the pandemic to promote all sorts of whacky theories that, just like flat earthers, were not grounded in science, facts, nor common sense. These theories were appealing especially at the beginning of the pandemic because we were extremely vulnerable and the whole situation was new for everyone. Nevertheless, these sorts of nonsensical conspiracy theories were recommended to innocent individuals, influencing some people to believe and then uphold such fallacious theories. This was not ideal at the beginning of the pandemic because it caused a lot of dissent among humanity, adding fuel to an already raging fire. Instead of worrying about collectively tackling the coronavirus head on through a united approach, conspiracy theorists were concerned about finding the "real" culprit, influencing other people to think the same. In a time when we needed real facts and solutions, conspiracy theorists were upsetting the apple cart with appealing theories. Their timing was off ethically, but an opportunity to be famous often outweighs what is ethical. The massive problem for social media companies, such as YouTube, was what was the best course of action ethically during the pandemic. In such a sensitive time, is it their duty to monitor and censor such theories to keep humanity centered on facts and the main concern of overcoming the virus? Well, that is what they did with some content (not that they haven't banned content prior to the pandemic). The problem for YouTube, and other social media platforms, is this course of action is against freedom of speech. This not only highlights inherent flaws within the fabric of social media, but also with the idea of freedom of speech itself. The question then should be, should such ill-informed views online be allowed to exist? Or should social media remain as the wild west? Should we be treating the online world differently to the offline world? Answering these questions is tricky. This is more of a socio-political problem that has no place in this book. But this problem is not isolated to conspiracy theories.

Infectious ideas have many disguises online. The whole "woke" mentality and ideology is based on infectious ideas and it is no coincidence that such a way of thinking was an outgrowth of social media. The whole woke cancel/outrage culture is the baby of social media. This self-righteous and misinformed ideology erodes democracy, not just in the West, but also in nations such as India, which destabilizes society leading to physical and psychological chaos.

Both conspiracy theories and woke cancel/outrage culture are only a few examples of how a dumb algorithm can influence people into believing infectious ideas. Ask yourself honestly, how has social media shaped your worldview? And more importantly, ask yourself this, would you have a different worldview if you were never influenced by social media? We all know the answer to both questions and it may be a bitter pill to swallow. But, in saying that, which worldview is the correct worldview? It is really more about common sense and what is factual and truthful that should be our worldview.

The Death of the Expert

Unfortunately, because of social media, we are encountering the death of the expert. I've encountered this personally, especially when people make up all sorts of unintelligible ideas about Eastern philosophy and spirituality when they disagree with my work. People will cite a five-minute YouTube video they watched about Taoism, for example, and think they know the tradition without ever reading the classical texts and extensive scholarly studies on Taoism.

People will disagree with an expert in a field with no prior training or thorough knowledge. This behavior is rife on social media. Anyone on social media can make up any sort of nonsense and if enough people believe it then that is the ammunition to discredit an actual expert's knowledge. People emotionally react online without ever fact checking their views or the expert's knowledge. I've encountered this irrational attitude so much on my YouTube channel that it could fill a warehouse. People will say, for example, "That is not what Hinduism is to me," and then they will explain what it is to them, which is just plain weird when you think about it. There is only what Hinduism is, not what it is to you. We are altering knowledge to suit ourselves. This is self-serving and self-interested behavior. But online it is so difficult to gain authentic knowledge when even big informational-based websites such as Wikipedia don't respect the expert, and as a result, spread misinformation. A great example is the 2019 NRL Grand Final (National Rugby League of Australia). During a pivotal moment in the game when the contest was in the balance, referee Ben Cummins made a terrible blunder when he signaled to the Canberra Raiders that they had six-again (a set of tackles in rugby league is six, giving the offensive team six opportunities to break the defensive line to score a try and when six-again is signaled it means the offensive team have another six opportunities to break the defensive line), only to retract his decision on the fly. The problem was the Canberra players, like everyone watching at home and in the crowd, thought it was six-again and the Canberra player got tackled under the impression that they had five more tackles in the set. But Cummins ordered a turnover to the confusion of everyone. As a result, the Sydney Roosters ran the length of the field a few moments later to score the match-winning try, which left a bitter taste in most fans' mouths.

After the game, I went to Wikipedia to look at Ben Cummins' profile. To my surprise, fans had already been hard at work changing his profile to include such untruthful statements as, "Ben 'Six-Again' Cummins is well known as the most incompetent ref in Australia. If the average worker performed like him they would be sacked." This statement is obviously not truthful, but this is the landscape of Wikipedia, a source for supposedly authentic knowledge based on the views of experts. How could anyone trust anything on Wikipedia?

Hindus especially have suffered from the misinformation on Wikipedia. A lot of Hindus have called out Wikipedia for their misinformation and have asked people to stop donating to them. But this is not just a Wikipedia problem, rather it is a problem with media in general, which is why "fake news" became a thing in the first place. Unfortunately, individuals within news media have certain biases that influence people and skew their worldview. The world got that complicated that even the media is not objective. How can a journalist call themselves a journalist when they are biased? Who can you trust?

Well, even though it appears that social media has killed the expert, the expert still exists in the shadows, but you have to get out of your own personal biases and prejudices and open your ears and listen and learn. To do so, you have to have discernment and think carefully before you consume content on social media. Make sure you fact check and don't believe someone just because they're articulate, charming, or have a lot of popularity. Social media doesn't care if the content you consume is true or beneficial for your psychological well-being. You are a resource for the algorithm to learn more about your behavioral patterns so that it can use them against you, building a state of mind within yourself that would have never been possible without the algorithm and the feedback loop.

From exploiting and influencing the behaviors of positive reinforcement and social approval, they are subtly fueling your addiction to the digital world. These behaviors drive addiction. But the tech industry could care less about your health and well-being.

Digital Addiction

To understand the widespread disease of digital addiction, we have to differentiate between behavioral and substance addictions. A substance addiction to alcohol or drugs (or any substance with psychoactive compounds) can directly change your brain chemistry, leading to a vicious dependency on a substance. Substance addiction was the only form of addiction considered until recent studies suggested otherwise. Appearing in the *American Journal of Drug and Alcohol Abuse* was an important survey paper in 2010 that concludes, "growing evidence suggests that behavioral addictions resemble substance addictions in many domains."[7]

We have to, as a result of such research, reframe our understanding of addiction to include both behavioral and substance addiction. Psychologists give us a clearer representation of how addictions should be understood:

Addiction is a condition in which a person engages in use of a substance or in a behavior for which the rewarding effects provide a compelling incentive to repeatedly pursue the behavior despite detrimental consequences.[8]

Yet to be clear, behavioral addictions are extremely moderate compared to strong chemical dependences people have for substances such as alcohol or drugs. Addictions to digital technology and substances are different. For example, if someone quits social media, they won't suffer the same withdrawal symptoms as someone with a strong chemical dependency. Nevertheless, behavioral addictions are quite detrimental to your health and well-being.

Someone with a behavioral addiction will feel helpless when checking your social media is only a tap of the screen away. It's just too hard to resist for most people. We are like a rabbit with a carrot dangling in front of it, we just can't resist the urge to try and get it. As I mentioned, positive reinforcement and social approval are evolutionary behaviors that are hard to kick. So, checking how many likes you got on a Facebook post is like getting a hit from a drug, however, it's not a substance we're addicted to but rather a behavioral pattern.

We constantly check social media to see how we are faring in our "apparent" worth to others (most of whom you likely don't know). We want to stay relevant and feel like we are needed by others. This seems to be a cup that is never full, it's never capable of satisfying you completely. But we constantly post and then anxiously monitor our social media accounts awaiting likes and retweets, and sometimes they never come. As a result, social media is more about vanity metrics than anything else, as we lean into those behavioral tendencies of positive reinforcement and social approval which the social media networks are exploiting. We are addicted to this feedback loop. We are gambling every time we post, but we aren't spending our money as we do with a slot machine, but instead our precious time and attention. The constancy of this feedback loop is dangerous for our health and sanity. It causes a lot of psychological problems that can threaten our life.

The Debt is Suicide

Suicide rates in general have increased a lot in recent years, where an estimated one million people worldwide die by suicide every year (in the last 45 years suicide rates have increased 60%). Especially with our youth. The main cause of suicide is mental illness, very commonly depression. And it's no surprise that rates in depression and self-harm are all up and it seems that it is hard to categorically point to one reason. But we might be a little too kind in our assessment.

Social psychologist Jonathan Haidt believes the main culprit is social media. Haidt explained on Joe Rogan's podcast that there is evidence of this with the exponential growth in major depressive episodes, psychological disorders, and non-fatal self-harm for young boys and girls, especially girls. The increase in rates are alarming. Haidt explains (for young people in America, Canada, and the UK) that the rates of depression and anxiety on average were fairly stable throughout the 90s and early 2000s. Haidt explains, "The percentage of kids aged 12 to 17 in America who met the criteria for having a major depressive episode... the rate for boys is around 5% and then around 2011 it starts going up and now it's around 7%."[9]

This is a substantial increase since the graph (Figure 7.1) Haidt was explaining only goes up to 2016, so 2% in five years is worrisome. But this is nothing compared to the increase with girls. Haidt explains, "The line for girls starts off higher because girls have more mood disorders, more anxiety and depression. Boys have more antisocial behavior, alcoholism, crime and violence... Girls basically make themselves miserable, boys make other people miserable."[10]

He continues, "The girls' rate is higher but it was stable from 2005 through 2010 and then right around 2011 and 2012 it starts going up, and it goes way up to the point where it goes up from about 12% to now about 20% of American teenage girls have had a major depressive episode in the last year, 1 in 5 [girls]."[11]

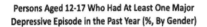

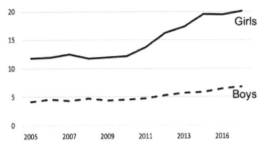

Persons Aged 12-17 Who Had At Least One Major Depressive Episode in the Past Year (%, By Gender)

Figure 7.1

Data from Higher Education Research Institute[12] (Figure 7.2) asked college men and women, do you have a psychological disorder (depression, etc.)? For the people who answered yes, the rates from 2010 to 2012 were low when it was millennials (Gen Y/ Generation Y): college men were on average 2-3%, while college women were about 5-6%. But then as iGen (Gen Z/Generation Z born in 1995 and after) began arriving at college in 2013, the rates began to skyrocket. From 2012 to 2016 men went from 2-3% to 6% and women went from 5-6% to a staggering 15% in a space of only four years. By 2016, college is almost all iGen'ers. This is extremely concerning considering the future of our world.

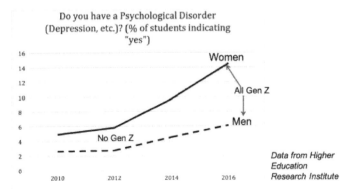

Figure 7.2

But there is another alarming and more extreme statistic[13] that Haidt produced on Joe Rogan's podcast. The statistics for young people deliberately harming themselves, which can be failed attempts at suicide, are deeply concerning. For boys and young men there is no real change in rates of non-fatal self-harm (as depicted in the graph in Figure 7.3). For all age groups the line is fairly steady.

Hospital Admissions for non-fatal self-harm: Boys

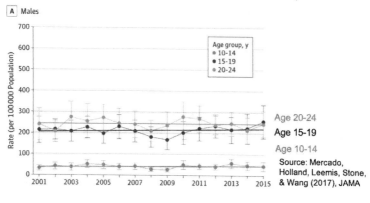

Figure 7.3

Hospital Admissions for non-fatal self-harm: Girls

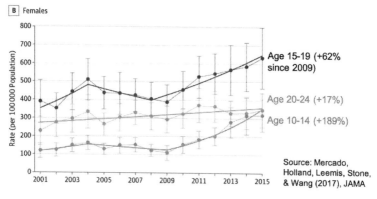

Figure 7.4

As for girls and young women admitted into hospital for deliberately harming themselves, there are some extremely concerning statistics (as depicted in the graph in Figure 7.4). Rates for millennial women aged 20-24 is up 17% from 2009 to 2015, which is alarming in itself. But the problems become really extreme with iGen'ers. We see a 62% increase of non-fatal self-harm with teenage girls aged 15-19. 62% from 2009 to 2015 is madness! Not to mention a statistic that shouldn't even be a topic of conversation, and that is the young age group of 10-14-year-old girls. Since 2009 there has been an increase of 189%. This is just not normal to have girls in their pre-teens harming themselves. Both boys and girls have never had this level of depression and anxiety in recorded history. Young people should never have a level of anxiety and stress equal or greater than an adult. So why is this? Why are our young people suffering so much?

The only new phenomenon in this timeframe, from 2009-2012, was the widespread use of social media as an application in smartphones. What else could these statistics be pointing to? Social media and the smartphone are the main culprits. And both are specifically affecting the wonderful women of the future (also men as well to a lesser degree). Haidt explains why girls specifically would suffer more from social media:

First look at the nature of aggression within the sexes. Boys' bullying is physical. Boys are physically dominating and then the risk is that they're going to get punched. So, you give everybody [boys] an iPhone, what do they do with it? Games and porn. They [boys] don't use it to hurt each other... Girls are actually as aggressive as boys. There's research from the eighties and nineties on this, if you include relational aggression girls don't bully each other by threatening to punch each other in the face, girls bully each other by damaging the other girl's social relationships, spreading rumors, spreading lies, spreading a doctored photograph, saying bad things, excluding them. It's relational aggression. And so, it's always been really hard to be a middle school student. It's always been harder to be a middle school girl than a middle school boy. So, beginning around 2010 and 2011 we throw in this brand-new thing into the mix, "OK, girls, here's this beautiful thing in your hand and here's all these programs where you can damage anyone's social relationships any time of the day or night with deniability from an anonymous account. Go at it girls!..." The nature of girls' bullying is hyper charged by social media and smartphones.[14]

Couple this with impossible beauty standards and the anxiety of being left out (which girls are extremely sensitive to), and you have a toxic recipe for psychological problems. This is all the result of behavioral addiction. And we have to be honest, there should be no reason why young people especially should be depressed, suffer from anxiety, or god forbid commit suicide. For this to happen there has to be something fundamentally wrong with society, and there is.

Our world hypnotically makes us believe that we should be "someone special" at all costs. Society itself is infected with the behaviors of positive reinforcement and social approval. As a result, our world promotes the idea of fame as a goal we should all chase. Television influenced this belief because the more eyeballs on you, the greater attention you attract and thus you have accomplished the goal of social approval. Your worth is apparently highly valuable. Social media has intensified this belief in fame at all costs. The "fame game" is *the* game being played on social media and we are gambling with our life.

We can all play social media lottery. But if you don't win (meaning getting a lot of likes and attention) you're a failure. This is not really true, but this is what the world would have you believe and social media promotes this illusion through vanity metrics. The way social media is designed influences people to seek fame as if it is important. Newsflash, fame is definitely not important and it shouldn't even be valued. You are perfectly fine just the way you are without any need for social validation. You need to push back on that tendency or face the dire consequences. And it's not only young girls who suffer from this, it's all of us.

People are doing all sorts of crazy and uncharacteristic things on social media just to get attention and be famous. People are eating pencils, being racist, spreading hate, painting with period blood, using their children as clickbait, and a host of other nonsense just so we attract attention. It's all insane. The more you behave like this, the less integrity you have.

Though, integrity and dignity don't seem to be high on many people's agenda these days. But both are virtues intrinsic to human nature. Fame, on the other hand, is an artificial creation of society. If we don't realize this before it's too late on an individual level, then the debt we accumulate can be a psychological weight that can lead people to suicide. This should never happen and social media should be held accountable, just like big tobacco were. But that is not likely going to happen in a world built around attracting attention. You, on an individual level, need to take ownership of your life and stop playing the fame game.

Many people suffer because other people are famous. Why not me, a lot of people ask. Social media influences this unnatural habit of comparing your life to others. We'll look at Instagram photos, watch YouTube videos, etc., and try and mimic a successful person's behavior or appearance to just get more eyeballs on us. We are under this liberal hypnosis that everyone is equal. We confuse equal rights, which are important, with equality of outcome, which can differ according to one's skillset. The truth is not everybody is equal, no matter what sort of liberal ideal someone is peddling. There are biological and psychological differences that we need to appreciate and respect. We need to understand that it is totally fine to have biological and psychological differences. In all seriousness, this should be obvious and not even a topic of conversation.

We live in an insane world when people are male, but they say they identify with being a female and we are supposed to believe that they are a woman. Absolute madness! Imagine if I said I am going to have a physique like Dwayne "The Rock" Johnson. I can try as hard as I want, I will never have the body of Johnson. He is naturally bigger boned and both he and I have psychological and genetic differences that make us better equipped for different vocations. He is built like a brick shithouse and I have the measly body of a writer. We need to respect these differences. But we live in a world now where I can just say that my body looks like Johnson's and you also have to believe that because you don't want to offend me, even though reality paints a completely different picture.

Yet social media influences people to be copycats in this game of fame. Why should Johnson be famous and massive and I'm not? This is not fair, people cry. This is the wrong attitude and what leads people into a negative view of oneself. You are beautiful and amazing without any of this bullshit. You don't need to be validated by anyone. If only our youth especially knew this. They wouldn't feel like a loser in a teenage jungle which can harm the best of us if we aren't aware that the fame game is pure bullshit. If someone is more popular and gets a lot of likes on Facebook, then good for them. It has nothing to do with you and it shouldn't affect you. Your life has its own journey.

Comparing your life to others on social media is not healthy because that life (the digital world) is not true. People strategically put snippets of their lives up to appear as a positive person living an awesome life. This can make you reflect on your own life and get you down. But it's an illusion and it's all part of the fame game. Those people who post positive snippets of their lives are just like you, they are seeking positive reinforcement and social approval. They are still comparing their lives to others, so they themselves try to portray a positive life. Don't be fooled by this game.

Accept that not everybody is equal. In the fame game there will always be those who are more popular than others. That is out of your hands. My advice is to stop playing this stupid game. Find your own lane in life and drive down that. That might not mean you'll be famous, but you'll be content because you held yourself with integrity and dignity by exploring what you are naturally drawn to, and not what social media makes you seek. You should never seek to be the center of attention, that is a psychological weakness and evidence of low self-esteem. It is insecure to want to be the topic of other people's conversations. Be fine with being nobody, and if fame comes, then so be it. Just remember fame isn't everything. But the design of social media makes you think otherwise and this is contributing to mental illnesses such as depression, self-harm, and suicide.

Social media wants us to be "somebody" and if we aren't then we will pay the ultimate price on our own if we don't wise up. We might want attention but attract none. Or worse, we could be cruelly bullied by trolls or other people, such as students who carelessly gang up on other students online. I'm not sure what social media's objective is here, but they surely must be aware that this is deeply affecting people. The suffering caused by social media needs to be addressed asap. And all of this suffering puts into jeopardy this whole notion that more connectivity is good.

More Connectivity is Bad for You
We are not naturally designed to deal with the amount of connectivity we have in our modern lives. It takes a lot of time

and effort to maintain a consistent dialogue on our Twitter, Facebook, Instagram, and YouTube accounts. We spend copious amounts of time replying to comments and messages as if it is our responsibility to do so. I've been accosted many times for replying to someone a few weeks later, and keep in mind on my network I don't know most of the people within it personally. So, it is strange to me when a stranger accosts me for not replying sooner. I have also been accosted by people I actually know as well. In both cases, it is strange to me. I have no obligation to monitor my social media accounts, nor do I have a phone capable of that.

You have no obligation to hurriedly reply to someone. But because the way digital technology has evolved, it is expected of us to be on the pulse all day long. This type of connectivity is new and not natural. Social media and apps like WhatsApp have enhanced this unnatural connectivity. This instant communication is expected of people, at least within their circle of friends and family.

This actually started before social media and the smartphone. I remember getting my first mobile phone when I was 21. I was living with three of my high school friends in Melbourne. A salesperson from Orange (a company now defunct) knocked on our door and sold us on a deal for four of the same mobile phones on a joint account (I know this type of deal sounds strange compared to these days). I never liked it from the get-go. It annoyed me that someone could ring or text me when I was out and about (this is several years before social media and the smartphone).

After some time I started leaving my phone at home when I would go to work or have my own leisure time. One of my friends I was living with took exception to my phone relationship. He tried to call me one day and he heard my phone ringing inside our house. When I arrived home, he was pissed and confronted me. He said and I quote, "What's the fucking point in having a phone if you're not going to keep it on you?" I thought what a whacky new world we live in. Keep in mind, why he "needed" to contact me was not important at all.

But he did have a point, why did I need a phone? I didn't, but I was young and unaware that I had a choice. Most people fall into this category because we are taught to follow social trends and what is expected of you is to have numerous amounts of communication devices so you can be reached at someone's beck and call. You actually become a slave to other people. I told that to my friend as well, "I am not your slave." Which he didn't understand at the time. But that is what we all become when people expect you to be as they want you to be. As Sherry Turkle points out:

> Phones have become woven into a fraught sense of obligation in friendship... Being a friend means being "on call" — tethered to your phone, ready to be attentive, online.[15]

Being "on call" is expected of us, from our friends and family. The idea of a constant digital dialogue frightens me personally. It is common for people to have some form of messenger (usually either SMS, iMessage, Facebook Messenger, or WhatsApp), where there is a continuous dialogue, polluted mainly with unnecessary messages and really, it's just a bunch of goofing around that wastes a hell of a lot of time. People try to justify this instant communication with a host of artificial concerns I mentioned earlier. But none of these hold up, considering the amount of time someone is distracted by and wastes in constant chitchat. This is a high price to pay considering that emergency you are eagerly awaiting may never come (thankfully).

Surely this is not the type of communication Samuel Morse envisioned when he unveiled the telegraph and tapped the phrase from the *Book of Numbers*: What hath God wrought? In its inception, instant communication was innocent. But then in less than 200 years we went from the telegraph to an anxious social media ping. Old-fashioned instant communication is different. When someone called your home telephone, one of your family members would take a message and pass the message onto you, where you might call them back later if necessary. There was no rush. People were far more patient because that's the way telecommunications were, so everything would get done in its own time. This sort of communication is stress-free.

The problem with smartphones, on the other hand, is that the instant communication capability is on a person at all times. On a moment's notice I can disturb you with a phone call or tweet or message and so on. Instead of having a private assistant taking messages for you, your private assistant is in your pocket, anxiously awaiting to deliver an annoying sound to you. This new form of instant communication anytime anywhere has made us a lot more impatient (as demonstrated by my friend).

We demand that people be at our beck and call, and if they don't play by the rules then watch out! Usually the person, like myself, who doesn't play the game becomes the source of instant communication in a group where the people are caught in a toxic cycle of cyber gossip. Don't be too perturbed if you are on the end of such gossip, your integrity and dignity are much more important than being in the "in" digital crowd. This power in numbers mentality is something people suffer from their whole lives. People feel secure in a group. Please don't fall into this trap. First of all, it is weak to feel secure in a crowd. Standing on your own two feet goes also for the decision you make in regards to digital technology. Have a little mystery, don't be so accessible. This will actually enrich your relationships because your time spent together is much more meaningful than a brief message on the phone here and there. Live an actual full-fledged life and don't let social trends hold you back.

The crowd always wants you to behave in a "normal" manner.

This is a red flag and something you should always avoid. But a big problem is from childhood we have this power in numbers mentality that is hard to shake for many in adulthood. This was a beneficial mentality as we evolved as a species, but it is an outdated mode of behavior. Yet instant digital communication is prolonging this behavior and enhancing its power.

As I mentioned earlier, all of this troll activity, cyber bullying, and ludicrous call-out culture is detrimental to the health and sanity of the world. This is most prevalent with our youth, as I discussed in regards to young girls and boys. Teenagers, especially, are running roughshod on social media. There is no filter and understanding that all of this online behavior is unhealthy. All of this connectivity allows teenagers access to someone's private life at the swipe of a screen. And those unfortunate teenagers who don't follow the crowd are wide open for malicious cyber-attack. This, as I mentioned earlier, leads to disastrous outcomes, such as depression, self-harm, suicide, and in some extreme cases gun shootings.

The human mind is so fragile, and we need better education and parenting to explain this to our youth. When I was a teenager, when there was a problem, we would sort it out on the playground face to face. Bullying can only go so far in the real world, but in the digital world it is an open slather. Digital connectivity is unnatural leading to unnatural results. I couldn't imagine what it would be like for teenagers in this digital world. It's hard enough being a teenager with all of the pressure of education and experiencing puberty to throw social media on top. This is a recipe for disaster.

Super connectivity is training our youth to be constantly agitated. It is doing this to adults as well, but it is something that a teenager or child shouldn't have to deal with. Cal Newport speaks about how our mind is hardly ever in solitude. This is what happens with hyper connectivity. We can't even go for a peaceful walk these days without our phone distracting us. Our mind is always engaged or anxiously awaiting to be engaged. Either way, the mind is on high alert without being relaxed.

Too much connectivity keeps our mind always moving. Our minds were not designed for this type of connectivity. We need to keep in mind that instant communication is not natural. So, to exist in this super connected world, we need to understand our mind. And our mind needs peace and quiet. It needs time to do *nothing*. But our world always tells us to be a go-getter. We should always be on the move; we should be on life's pulse. This type of modern attitude is killing us. Our mind has no time to breathe. We are 24/7 connected and people find it hard to unplug. We are cramming an unhealthy amount of information in our heads.

Our nervous system is not designed for constant mental activity or this amount of stimulation. The anxiety is at such a high level that our fight-or-flight switch is stuck in the *on* position (in Part III I will discuss this more at length and how we can switch off the fight-or-flight switch and relax the nervous system). This is terrible for anyone, but especially for our youth. Young people aren't ready for this type of anxiety. Only adults used to experience chronic stress and anxiety, but now it is common for young people, which is contributing to mental health problems in young people. Our minds are not designed for this much stimulation. All of this connectivity will lead to an undesirable future for generations to come. We have to address this problem now. There needs to be a radical evaluation of social media and digital technology use for young people.

Social Media and Smartphones 18+

My radical solution to the problems teenagers and children have from using digital technology is to make them for people 18 years of age and over (18+). The epidemic of social media and smartphones (not to mention other digital devices) are causing a lot of bad health and insanity around the world. It's best for all age groups to monitor their use. I guess for all adults it's a case of "you're old enough to know better" in the same way adults have a choice to abuse alcohol or not. But young people don't have the life experience to know what is detrimental to their health and sanity. And, as we see with growing suicide rates, the way teenagers are using social media and smartphones is not positive.

Anything that is not good for our health is often labeled 18+. When people finally comprehended that alcohol and cigarettes were bad for their health, they slapped an 18+ label on them and just let adults make their own choices (unless you're in the Indian states of Bihar, Gujarat, Mizoram, Nagaland, and the Union Territory of Lakshadweep, where alcohol is banned). Let's hope that an 18+ designation for social media and smartphones won't take as long as it did with cigarettes and alcohol. Even though many people, especially parents and tech companies, will push back on my suggestion, we have to call a spade a spade and come to the conclusion that they are both detrimental to our health and sanity, so young people should be shielded from them until they are old enough to know better.

The main obstacle is how we implement such a law. It has to begin on a social level, a general understanding that both social media and smartphones are bad for you in excess, as happened with alcohol and cigarettes. This will be pushed along when this understanding filters into government. It realistically has to begin with government policy. This would hopefully drive change. The next hurdle would be the tech industry. They would have to assume some responsibility and ban young people under the age of 18 from owning a smartphone or having a social media account. There needs to be strict policies as with alcohol and cigarettes to outlaw young people from the digital world.

The last obstacle are parents. This could be easy or difficult for some parents, depending on how responsible they are.

Parents need to understand, as with alcohol and cigarettes, social media and smartphones are not good for their child's health and sanity. You wouldn't light up a few cigarettes and crack a cold beer with your kids, so this way of thinking needs to be projected onto social media and digital technology. If we care about our children, then we'll block them from using social media and smartphones. Yet the tech companies could intervene and create some sort of technology where the device knows who is using it and if it is someone under 18 then it won't allow them to use it. I'm not sure what that sort of technology blocking system looks like, but I have no doubt it could be created. This would take the hassle of parents constantly monitoring their children out of the equation. With all that said, the tech industry would push back on such a policy because it would hurt their economic bottom line. And this could also influence a government's thinking as well, since a lot of young people have smartphones. But in the end, it is our responsibility to future generations to choose their health and sanity over and above the economy. We can't confuse a man-made system over reality itself. If we continue to be fooled by such illusions then we cannot blame the world for becoming dumber and dumber. The unconscious use of social media and digital devices is diminishing our intelligence.

Digital technology is slowly making us dumber without us understanding that this is happening. We've been hypnotized by digital technology because it has the ability to take us away from the reality of our lives. Our mind is confused to the point that we want to be machines ourselves. Here is a newsflash, you will always be human so deal with it. We have stopped acting like humans because we are mimicking the machines we are addicted to. You are human, the greatest piece of technology on the planet. We have to minimize the time we spend on digital devices to realize our humanity. We need to reclaim our mind if we want to live in a healthy and sane world.

Part III

Reclaim Your Nature to Live in a Healthy and Sane World

Chapter 8

The Perfect Technology is Human

In this third part of the book you will learn the tools, strategies, and wisdom to reclaim your mind from technology so that we can eventually live in a healthy and sane world. First of all, as I've mentioned throughout the book, we have to accept that the human condition is in a suboptimal state because our lives are consumed with technology, usually the digital screen variety.

The health and sanity of the world are being diminished because of our addiction to digital technology. We cannot rely on the tech companies to clamp down on their approach to engage your attention through clever algorithms all personally designed to distract you and lock you into their world. The onus and responsibility are leveled directly at you. No one else will help you, especially since the majority of people are hypnotized by the digital world's influence. You need to pull your own bootstraps up. You will learn how to do this in this final part of the book. To claim our life back, we first need to understand the greatest piece of technology in the known universe.

Human Technology

We've traversed to the depths of technology, giving us our modern convenience and all the new digital devices that consume our time. This is a bottomless pit which continues to fascinate us as the newest digital adaptations are the trend. But this focus on the possibilities and eventual inventions of technology has come at a price. We have forgotten about the most sophisticated piece of technology in the known universe, the human being.

The majority of people alive right now don't even understand their own human technology. We live our life not conscious of the magnitude and immensity of what it is to be in a human body. People are actually desensitized to their own psychosomatic organism, which is evident in the food they shovel in their mouths and the amount of useless entertainment that pollutes their eyes and ears. This type of lifestyle trains our mind to be unconscious. This unconscious state, resulting from years of distractions, feels most comfortable for most people.

The trained habit of overstimulating our mind and body is causing this hypnosis. We have become accustomed to "vegging out." From a young age we learn to sit in front of a television, or these days a smartphone or tablet, and this unknowingly trains ourselves to be unconscious. Parents continue to let the world down in this regard. Parents should never put their children in front of a screen in infancy, or at all, at least until children become old enough to make their own decisions.

Many parents understand this problem, but they usually make up excuses such as how hard it is to be a parent. These sorts of empty and selfish excuses frustrate me. If you are an aspiring parent and do not want to assume responsibility then please don't have children, we are overpopulated as it is so this might be your most noble act. If you are a parent then eliminating screens from your child's life will be beneficial long-term, not just for the child but also for the health and sanity of the entire world. As a parent you would be doing a great service for humanity. If parents could make this decision then the next generation might have a chance of being more conscious and they would be able to rewrite the wrongs of our generation. But we still have a chance, even if you are a millennial or an iGen'er who knows no different than the digital world.

Eliminate Unconsciousness

We have to eliminate our daily habit of unconsciousness. Most of the time we yearn for this distracted state because it momentarily takes us away from our lives. We will get home from a long day at work and just want to gorge on food while we watch our favorite programs. I can sympathize with people yearning for this down time because I too have been there. But this habit is part of the problem. Something I had to realize as well once upon a time.

The way to eliminate unconsciousness and its distractive tendency is to increase consciousness. The simple method to increase consciousness is to be more conscious. I'm not referring to having more information and knowing a lot of things, though that may help. What I am referring to is attention, pure attention. Pure attention is the natural ability to be completely present in the moment without thoughts, anxiety, or stress interfering (this state is referred to in the East as pure consciousness).

Pure attention is our natural state of mind. Before life touches our mind, and we subsequently go through all the conditioning that comes with socialization, our attention is unstained. In the great Eastern traditions, their focus is to return to this pure state because that is who we truly are. Being conscious, then, is to be purely aware of reality without our view of it skewed by our conditioning. In this pure state you perceive reality as it is without your idea of "what" it is. The way to increase this state of consciousness is to decrease our unconscious habit of overstimulation. Overstimulation causes unconsciousness and then our addiction to this behavior. We have to be honest with ourselves without letting our addiction fool us into believing this habit is normal. It's not. You have to honestly pinpoint how much time you spend in unconsciousness.

Do you come home from work and waste your precious time? The consensus answer is yes. Though you have leaned into distraction as some sort of savior *from* your life, it's actually your enemy. The reason we don't understand our human technology is because we neglect it. For us to understand our human technology, we have to unravel it from everything that keeps us from reaching our true potential.

Distracting ourselves, especially through digital devices, has never been considered a problem. But this tendency to distract ourselves is harming us and causing long-term psychological problems. Unconsciousness comes from being overly distracted, and distraction comes from habitual overstimulation. Our mind is extremely agitated, with the inner volume turned right up. We are like speakers with the volume turned up to the max. Leaving the volume in this position is going to cause permanent damage to the speakers. Speakers with the volume turned up permanently lose contact with their base resonance which is silence. That is until the speakers explode. Our mind is the same. If our inner volume is at max resulting from overstimulation and distractions, then we will break down eventually. This unfortunate breakdown looks like chronic anxiety and stress, depression, mental health issues, and suicide, just to name a few.

The majority of people's mental volume in the world is running at max and we lose sight and feeling of our base resonance which is pure attention. And pure attention is calm, serene, and peaceful. We cannot know our original state if we are constantly consuming distractive stimulation.

How We Consume Energy

To understand human technology, we need to understand the energy that fuels it. We consume energy in three main ways, the air we breathe, the food and liquid we ingest, and the sense impressions we take in through our eyes and ears.

In the East, they explain how important it is to our health and well-being to be conscious of how we consume these three energies. All three have the potential to affect the body and mind on a subtle level. Air is a tricky one considering a growing population now live in cities. Though, the air we breathe is not equally efficacious as the other two energies considering the human condition and how to operate human technology properly. But if you have a chance to live in nature away from cities then this will be beneficial for long-term health.

The food we ingest and sense impression, on the other hand, are primary when it comes to understanding human technology. If both are carelessly taken care of then this contributes to further unconsciousness because our fuel choice for both is invariably toxic. Both contribute to how our mind is functioning, our basic sanity. Most people don't think that the food they eat and what they drink affects the mind. Well it does. Often an agitated and restless mind results from bad dietary choices. If you consume a lot of heavy carbs, caffeine, sweets, and overly spicy food then your mind will be subtly agitated with the inner volume beginning to reach max. Eating this type of food too regularly is disastrous. Yet most are accustomed to this feeling because of junk food and processed food.

These sorts of food choices don't just keep your mind in an agitated state, but also lead to a host of other health issues. As for what we drink, well it's a no-brainer. Alcohol, caffeinated beverages, and sugary drinks overstimulate our nervous system leading to an unsteady mind. You can't know yourself deeply or your fundamental human technology if you are constantly consuming these sorts of beverages.

Anything that ramps up your alertness and makes your mind restless is something to be avoided, especially if we want to be fully conscious. These types of food and beverage choices are distractions themselves which lead to overstimulation. Distractive foods are like the busyness of social media and healthy food is simple just like basic e-mail. But people find e-mail boring and want to spice it up with useless busyness on social media. These tendencies expose our greed. We often want too much and our culture is built on excess. Having too much or too many choices is not healthy for our body and mind.

Our food choices need to be simplified if we are to gain control of our own organic technology. Because of the illusory belief in mind-body dualism, we incorrectly believe that the stomach (gut) and brain are two isolated organs. The truth is the gut and brain are a unified system, and this needs to be respected if we want to cease our unconscious lives. Agitating the mind through the gut is an indirect method leading us into unconsciousness (learn more about healthy dietary choices in my book *Emotional Intuition for Peak Performance*).

The direct path, and what is the focus in this book, is the fuel we take in through the eyes and ears. In fact, our eating choices are lazy and poor because often the entertainment we take in through the eyes and ears is our priority. This is backwards. So much of our lives now are focused on being entertained and this is a big reason why the digital world is slowly taking over our minds. Entertainment pacifies the mind, which is the attraction for us if we want a reprieve from our daily lives. Digital devices have provided instant gratification for entertainment, news, and communication. At the beginning this instant gratification was thought of as beneficial, but it has turned out to be harmful.

Being constantly plugged into the digital world causes our mind to be chronically anxious because our fight-or-flight switch is stuck in the *on* position. We cannot know ourselves or take care of our human technology in this anxious state. We have to truly understand why the overconsumption of digital technology is harmful. When we examine our psychosomatic organism (human technology) we are an upside-down tree, as philosopher, social reformer, architect, and esotericist Rudolf Steiner suggested. The branches of our nervous system take in experience and we then feel the effects in our mind. How does this happen?

In vertebrate species, such as human beings, the nervous system contains two parts, the central nervous system (CNS) and the peripheral nervous system (PNS). The central nervous system contains the brain and spinal cord, while the peripheral nervous system consists of mainly nerves, which are enclosed bundles of long fibers, and axons, which are long, slender projections of nerve cells that conduct electrical impulses away from the neuron's cell body. These nerves and axons connect the central nervous system to every other part of the body. The peripheral nervous system is divided into the somatic nervous system (SoNs) and the autonomic nervous system (ANS). The autonomic nervous system is our main focus when it comes to the harmful effects of digital technology.

The autonomic nervous system has two branches: the sympathetic nervous system (SNS) and the parasympathetic nervous system (PSNS). The sympathetic nervous system is sometimes considered the "fight-or-flight" system because it is activated in cases of emergencies to mobilize energy. It is what we activate when we are in motion and being stimulated through our senses. Without it we could not *do* anything. The parasympathetic nervous system, on the other hand, is often considered the "rest and digest" or "feed and breed" system because it is activated when we are in a relaxed state. We activate the parasympathetic nervous system when we essentially do *nothing*. It is also responsible for stimulation of "rest and digest" and "feed and breed" activities that occur when the body is at rest, especially after eating, including sexual arousal, lacrimation (tears), salivation, urination, digestion, and defecation. The parasympathetic nervous system is what makes us drift off to sleep every night. It is stimulated most when we relax deeply.

In our world we have overcompensated for the sympathetic nervous system. We are constantly doing something which depletes our energy reserves. And when I say "doing" something, I don't just mean in the physical active sense. People mistake activity for only physical actions. The evidence of this is when people have time to relax, or state that they want to relax, they log onto their digital devices. When it's time to relax, if you sit in front of a TV or play with your phone then you are still not relaxing. Actually, you are activating the sympathetic nervous system.

When you are consuming digital devices through the eyes and ears you are still activating the sympathetic nervous system which agitates the mind, even if you are comfortable on your couch. When we overstimulate our sympathetic nervous system our fight-or-flight response is stuck in the on position. No wonder people are stressed out. To counter this nervous system response, we need to access the parasympathetic nervous system.

The parasympathetic nervous system is not only activated when we sleep. It is also important to activate it in waking hours as well. Instead of running away from boredom by filling it up with mindless entertainment, we should embrace boredom and sit with it. Boredom is only a response we feel when we have become too accustomed with filling our mind up with activity, essentially overstimulating the sympathetic nervous system. Sitting quietly in our boredom trains us to access the parasympathetic nervous system.

Sitting meditation is also an effective method for accessing the parasympathetic nervous system. Actually, more time spent in meditation over a long period of time is sufficient enough to restore our needed daily dose of activating the parasympathetic nervous system. A thirty-minute morning meditation practice will nourish your active intellectual life all day, just that small dose. If you add another thirty minutes before bed or increase the duration of daily meditation then the benefits will be maximized. On top of these two methods, obviously spending as much time away from digital devices is positive (I will explain strategies to decrease your digital consumption next chapter). Constantly engaging with digital devices keeps your mind in an active and unconscious state. A new view on how we use technology for our benefit is needed.

System Override

When we understand that the human organism is the most sophisticated technology in the known universe then we will begin to treat it that way. But we sadly neglect our own technology and are more interested in digital technology. We spend all sorts of money to insure digital devices run optimally. We'll install an antivirus on our computer or cleaning software for our smartphone, but we don't show the same careful attention to ourselves. Instead of installing our own personal antivirus, we continually upload viruses in our mind that corrupt our system. For this habit to stop we have to be conscious of what we are uploading, what we are taking in through our eyes and ears.

We can't continue to activate the sympathetic nervous system and proclaim that we are healthy and sane. The way to counter this is to ease the burden on yourself by activating the parasympathetic nervous system. The only way to do this is by decreasing the amount of information we consume. With the Internet came the new phenomenon of informational overload. We can jump from one subject to the other on the Internet, and though we thought this was brilliant in the beginning, it's completely disastrous because too much information fragments our mind and takes it to a new level of restlessness we've never experienced before in our evolution. Our brains are not designed to consume too much information.

We've all studied a few subjects before bed and then toss and turn for hours trying to get to sleep. This is similar to sometimes when we close the laptop to see that it is still on with certain programs running keeping it active. We are the same; if we take in too much information before bed, when we close our eyes that information is still rattling around inside our skull blocking us from needed sleep. This informational multitasking causes a lot of anxiety and stress, leading to other worse mental health issues because our brain is not designed to go back and forth from one piece of information to another. Our mind simply cannot keep up. To overhaul our system, we need to turn off this constantly running informational tap, not just before bed but all throughout the day. It's completely fine not to know everything.

We live in a culture where we need to keep up with the Joneses with all current information. The problem with people trying to stay on the informational pulse is no one can know anything deeply. It becomes all soundbites and surface information that we parrot to one another as if we know it all deeply. This is like having a thousand small files on your computer that are scattered everywhere containing only a small bit of information, like a word document multiplied by 1000. These one thousand files could never be large and subsequently when we view one of those files it only has a small bit of information on it. A mind with one thousand small word document files is not running optimally, as there are too many files with only tidbits of information in them.

A computer with minimal files and software allows the hard drive to run optimally. We are the same. Instead of too much surface information and daily input bouncing around in our mind, we could have less information that we are more knowledgeable about. People who are wise or skillful usually have zeroed in on one or two particular knowledge streams where they center their informational input. This deepens their knowledge and they know their particular subject or skill very deeply.

Many people wonder how other people become great, well that's the secret, don't overload your mind with too much unnecessary information. You need to delete all the useless information, especially information you don't know thoroughly. It's all useless and taking up too much mental storage. On top of this you need to reduce the amount of information you take in, unless it is part of your knowledge stream. Nourishing our own knowledge stream requires us to consume educational information rather than useless unconscious entertainment.

Educational information is like clean software while entertainment is corrupted software that will affect your entire system.

If we become more mindful of what too much information does to us, we will only take in the information that benefits our health and sanity as well as what is needed for your particular knowledge stream (mine being Eastern philosophy). You have to learn to guard what comes in through your eyes and ears (next chapter I will discuss methods to help this protection). The more you guard your eyes and ears the more protection your mind has. This allows for more activation of the parasympathetic nervous system. You will begin to be calmer and more present without the effects of stress and anxiety inhibiting your experience.

When you reside in the parasympathetic nervous system state more frequently old unnecessary information and unneeded memories begin to be deleted from your mind. As this process continues your mind becomes much more settled and you will have a sense of space or ease inside your head. This is like deleting a lot of software from a computer leaving the hard drive with a lot of space to run smoothly. When we leave only a few programs inside our head we begin to access a dimension of mind most people don't believe exists.

Your True Nature is Blissful

The more we turn off our digital devices and spend time in quietude and inactivity, accessing the parasympathetic nervous system, the more we come into contact with our true nature. Our nature is beneath an agitated mind and the humdrum of society. What is beneath the overactive and overstimulated mind? *Bliss*, unassociated bliss. The core of human technology is unassociated bliss or joy and real happiness in other words. This bliss dwells within each of our minds. But it is not accessed through overstimulating our mind.

You cannot always be on digital devices and experience bliss. It only happens when the mind is completely rested regularly in the parasympathetic nervous system. It can happen no other way. People mistakenly believe they will experience bliss through pleasure. We fill our mind and belly up full of pleasurable stimuli, but it always leaves us empty and wanting more. We can never experience bliss through pleasure.

Bliss is an aspect of our mind beneath pleasure seeking. Bliss, then, happens of itself when we decrease overstimulating ourselves. Bliss is not dependent on pleasure; it is innate within us which is something the great Eastern spiritual traditions figured out experientially through deep contemplation and meditation. The bad health and sanity of our world are not caused by intrinsically bad people, but rather overstimulated people driven by a society whose ethos is to stay busy with a go-get-them attitude. We will never experience bliss with this attitude. You might take pride in your busyness, say if you're an entrepreneur, but you will never be blissful. And because we have sold ourselves on the belief that overstimulation is natural, joy is missing from the world (in case you haven't noticed). Though you want to stay plugged into the social media world, the truth is you will never be truly happy. Your mind will continue to be agitated which eclipses the bliss in your mind.

Individually living in a blissful state is the greatest contribution you could give to the world. Bliss is our fundamental nature, but digital technology opposes it. You will never be happy trying to get more attention on social media, it's a fleeting experience. This only contributes to an insane world. Bliss, true unassociated happiness, is the purest health and sanity we can experience. Your nature is blissful. But you will never experience it if you continue down this unnatural path of allowing your mind to be continually distracted by the digital world. We need strategies and tools to combat the digital world or we will never experience true happiness and live in a healthy and sane world.

Chapter 9

A Digital-Free Lifestyle

Throughout this book I've explored the impact digital technology is having on us and how in most cases it is of a negative consequence. Now that we understand the human being is the most sophisticated technology in the known universe, it is time to understand how to operate our system at an optimal level. For us to be at our optimal level requires us to drastically reduce our use of digital technology or to eliminate it altogether. If we don't choose either then we run the risk of doing real psychological damage as we continue to lead very unproductive lives.

If you want to live an optimal life so you can live in a healthy and sane world, then you need to consciously say a loud and clear NO to digital technology ruling your life. To do so we need strategies and methods that will promote a digital-free lifestyle.

Stop Fidgeting, You're an Adult

When I see people constantly reaching for their phones and mindlessly playing with them, it reminds me of when we were all children and we had the bad habit of fidgeting with things that usually our parents curbed over time. But it seems that our fidgeting past has reared its ugly head with adults through digital technology. I am stunned when I see people walking and looking at their phones or when people are eating together and they play with their phones without making eye contact or conversation.

From the moment people wake up they are fidgeting with their phones. Even trusted intellectuals in the field of neuroscience admit to checking their phone on waking up. They definitely should know better and it makes it hard to trust "scientists" with such behavior. To counter this behavior, your first order of business should be that you never leave your phone in your bedroom or use it as an alarm. Using a phone as an alarm is just an excuse to leave it in your bedroom while it entices you to play with it. Buy a traditional alarm clock and leave the phone turned off in another room until it is absolutely necessary to turn it on. This one habit will reduce anxiety and improve sleep. This act states how important it is to prioritize sleep, rather than firing off that last tweet in bed which keeps you up for hours. Habitually leaving your phone out of the bedroom improves your quality of life. It requires you to stop fidgeting like a child and prioritizing what is important.

When you leave home, you need to train yourself to leave your phone in your pocket or bag on silent so it doesn't distract your journey from A to B. You'll be surprised how much of life is missed on our simple journeys. What will help this is if you can disengage the Internet on your phone and delete all the social media apps and any other apps that are not necessary (from all of these years not having a smartphone I'm not sure if any apps are necessary). Modifying your phone in this way will decrease your attraction for using the phone mindlessly as you get from A to B. This will stop you from walking and looking at your phone, which really is dangerous. Not to mention how this will help people avoid playing with their phone while they drive which is still a habit a lot of people do even with all the laws in place to prevent such dangerous actions.

When you walk, ride a bike, or drive, you should be paying attention to what is going on around you rather than some artificial world. When our attention is distracted then that distraction takes priority over everything else. Think of Neo in *The Matrix* when his attention is distracted by the woman in the red dress. This is extremely important when we examine our face-to-face interactions with the nosey smartphone looming over our conversations.

We've all been in a conversation when someone has their phone in their hand or on their desk or dinner table. What this symbolizes to other people is the phone is the most important thing, not you. You might discuss a project with your boss and their phone is sitting on the desk waiting to ring which distracts the boss and illustrates to you that you are of secondary importance. This is best demonstrated at the dinner table. It's more common now to see a whole family or friends eating together but making no eye contact because they are all playing with their phones. Why eat together in the first place? I feel embarrassed for people when I see this sort of behavior. If you are one who is guilty of this behavior then you are subtly telling your friends and family that they are not as important as this illusionary life you are living in the digital world.

Over the years I've developed a method to counter such behavior. If I am with someone and we are talking and they get distracted by their phone and want to keep talking, as if they are listening, I will just stop talking until they are finished on their phone. Often people feel uncomfortable when I do this, but imagine how I feel taking a backseat in a conversation to an inanimate object. Imagine you were talking to somebody and someone else started having a discussion with them at the same time and they were juggling between both conversations. Well that is what is happening when someone is playing with their phone and talking to you at the same time.

When I have a conversation with somebody, they have my undivided attention. I don't have an active phone with all the bells and whistles, so no one will have that problem with me. My approach allows for more fruitful conversations that are pure. But if you choose this method then having your phone on the table facing screen down is not good enough. Having a phone on the table still symbolizes its importance over the other people you are engaging with. Your phone should be on silent or turned off in your pocket, bag, or better yet left at home so it can't bother you. And people will argue, what if someone wants to contact them? My answer is, why can't it all wait until you are home? And how often seriously has someone "really" needed to contact you? Not much, considering a lot of online banter is still the same chitchat nonsense many people engage in.

We create these artificial concerns to justify our smartphone's existence. Everyone uses the old line, "What if there is an emergency?" as if we need to be sensitive to this possibility. But seriously, how often has a real emergency popped up? (And I don't mean calling your spouse to pick up something for dinner.) Other people will try and justify their smartphone's existence because they feel they will miss out on an important event in someone's life. For example, if your friend is pregnant and she is awaiting the birth of her child, you don't want to miss her Instagram photos so you can send her a heart icon. Sounds ridiculous right? But that's the world we live in, seriously! You know what's better than sending a silly social media comment or like, actually putting aside the time to visit them, or if you live far away, set aside some time to have a Skype conversation on your computer, not on your phone. Make the effort, your friend deserves it.

In all cases, these artificial concerns are not tangible concerns. They are just our imagination running wild to justify our bad phone habit. You don't have to keep up with the Joneses and be on the pulse of every tidbit of information in people's lives or worldly affairs. If someone as famous as Hollywood director Christopher Nolan doesn't have a phone or e-mail then I'm sure you definitely don't need to stay plugged in all the time. You're not that famous.

You don't need your phone on you at all times, especially when you are going to meet people. Having a phone on you causes subtle anxiety because it could ring or make a social media ping any time. Walking around anxious or even worse feeding that anxiety by fidgeting with your phone is not healthy. Comparing the digital world to the natural world is no competition. The natural world is much more fascinating, but we've bought into this illusionary world. It sustains our childish fidgeting habit. To counter this, we not only need to stop fidgeting with our phone, but we also need to lose our attraction for what is in the digital world.

Reduce Online Activity

Reducing our childish fidgety habits is dependent on reducing our online activity. A reduction in online activity can only happen, for most, when we lose our attraction to what is in the digital world. This goes much deeper than just having a bad habit; it is more so to do with how we are within our mind and who we also secretly want to be.

Our addictive attraction to the digital world reveals many deep-seated psychological problems a lot of people have but have never addressed. We can only deal with those problems if we reduce our online activity. If you are sincere and want to be healthy and sane so you can live in a healthy and sane world then you have to reduce your online time drastically if you wish to deal with your deep-seated problems. First, we need to deal with the number one source of online addiction, social media.

The Trap of Social Media

We've become so consumed with the world of social media that we've lost contact with our real social self. We have fallen for vanity metrics, as we anxiously await the next "like" on our Facebook post, for example. We depend so much on what people think of our digital persona. Though, we could say this is not even a persona, as social media has largely become about who can cause the most drama and noise to attract the most attention and followers. This is quite a unique phenomenon.

Most people, then, have their real lives and then they have this digital life where they want to get noticed and gain people's attention. Most people in their normal lives work an average job where attracting attention is not so important. A famous person, on the other hand, is 24/7 about attracting attention and social media has magnified this ability for them. The problem for the majority of social media users is they aspire to have the same level of fame in the digital world as a famous person in reality (though they're probably not ready for that level of fame because it comes at a price). Social media has revealed that people are desperate to become famous and they'll do anything to get fame, even if it means becoming someone else.

The Cult of Comparison

Trying to be somebody else is driven by comparing our lives to others. We'll see a famous person's or a friend's social media presence, which showcases the wonderful life they *appear* to be living and we'll do our best to replicate that life even if we know we are truly sad. For example, we'll alter our images on Instagram to get attention and this is completely dishonest. We want to look a certain way, but in reality, we don't look anything like the images we are altering. We might have some natural blemishes on our face, but we will digitally alter them to look apparently pretty.

People follow someone like actor Dwayne "The Rock" Johnson on Instagram and they envy his physique and positive attitude (as if he is positive all the time, which he's not). For example, instead of appreciating Johnson's path and work ethic, people will go to any length to replicate his life or shower him with undeserving adulation. People focus too much on external appearance and think this is the foundation of life. It's not. The problem is you've been duped into believing the material world is all there is and you've forgotten that consciousness is the foundation of life. How we are within is far more important than how we look on the outside. And because we only value the material world, we want to have that pretty face or fantastic body some famous person may have, which actually has been altered itself (we will also sadly envy and compare our lives to our friends as well).

People will do anything to have a great body and the perfect face. Look at the growing boom in the plastic surgery industry. For example, women want Angelina Jolie's lips or Nicole Kidman's nose and they will destroy their face to have them. But nothing looks more fake than a fake face and a silly skinny and pointy nose. Men, on the other hand, will also do anything to have a chiseled body. They will take steroids, inject their muscles with oil, and waste too much time in a gym lifting weights. All of these alterations are driven by comparison. We have an image in our mind of what is perfect and we'll do anything to get there. Social media enhances this problem. We alter our real life to look a certain way for other people. But if you're intelligent, you know it's all a sham.

Those who are comparing their lives to others are the unhappiest people in the world. Constantly looking at other people's lives and comparing yours leads to mental health issues such as depression. People feel depressed when they see all the wonderful things other people are doing, but they just don't know that all of these shiny social media lives are based on a lie. You are only seeing a version of someone else's life that they want you to see, which has actually been altered anyway. It's all a sham.

The best medicine to cure this problem is to delete your social media accounts or at least follow people you actually know (like real-life friends) rather than famous people. Remember that those famous people are just as insecure as normal people when it comes to comparison. Actually, their problems are likely much, much worse. Probably the biggest problem with comparison on social media is you end up with an unhealthy psychological split between who you truly are and the digital persona you put out there for other people to see. This is psychologically damaging because we end up with this unnatural phenomenon of having two selves.

Delete Your Social Media Ego

Having two selves is not sane. As I mentioned earlier in this book, I've met a lot of people from social media in the real world and they are nothing like who they pretend to be online (probably because they are in the business of vanity metrics). It is not sane to portray a digital social media persona and then be somebody else in the real world. If you fall into this category then this is not psychologically healthy. You could be spreading messages of peace but be a complete asshole or vice versa. It doesn't matter either way because if you are being two people then this is not sane.

If you exhibit any of these tendencies then I'd suggest you permanently delete your social media presence. This would be far healthier for you in the long run and something realistically we should all consider eventually. But even if your normal self is the one you portray on social media, it is still beneficial to reduce your activity or delete it if you feel compelled to do so. If you can't have a healthy relationship with social media then you need to consider your options. We all don't know how to use social media because it is so new. Our lower drives tend to proliferate the social media world. People yearning for fame, showcasing their wealth and greed, and being a drama farmer are all the behaviors we have regressed into and wrongly believe have value.

Imagine if you used social media moderately, not for vanity metrics but instead to educate and inspire. In the end, social media only has value if it is educational and inspirational, everything else including your digital persona is pointless as it could all be taken away if the social media companies went bankrupt. We are like children who neglect their toys. Social media could be beneficial but we're using it to fulfill our lower urges. It's up to us to use it intelligently or delete it altogether. If you used it intelligently for educational reasons you wouldn't feel an urge to look at your phone every five seconds because vanity metrics are taken out of the equation (though don't pretend to educate and inspire in disguise to get attention).

If you use social media for educational purposes most of your posts will be about something other than yourself. Social media is too often neglected by people posting things about themselves which fuels vanity metrics. This one reason is why I stayed away from social media for many years. I used to call Facebook "Egobook" because it seemed that many people were only interested in talking about themselves and fame, which is sadly true. If you are one of the many who suffer from vanity metrics then you have to either choose sanity or delusion. You might not think that your two-persona habit is inherently unhealthy, but it will cause long-term psychological problems. And if someone did need medical attention later on from social media use, you can bet your bottom dollar that the big social media companies are not going to compensate them. We already see this behavior towards people who have Internet addiction, no company is willing to help at any extreme length. Keep in mind, Steve Jobs prohibited his kids from using the iPad because of digital technology's addictive powers. Also, Bill Gates implemented a cap on screen time for his kids. If the two biggest tech figures in recent history don't allow their children to overly use digital technology, why should you use it at all?

In a day our online activity should be very limited because real life is where we really exist. Sadly, many people spend more time online than offline these days. Keeping that fake online persona relevant takes a lot of work. Reverting back to real life can be done by deleting your social media ego or by drastically reducing your presence and time spent on it. If you think you can have a social media presence and use it intelligently then it is important you don't fall for the traps that are laid out for you.

Especially those traps set by trolls.

Don't Engage with Trolls

People waste a lot of time defending their posts against trolls who have nothing better to do than cause unnecessary drama. Again, if you are a troll shame on you. In the real world people may disagree in an intelligent way because social cues are still in play. But online the playbook is thrown out by trolls, as it becomes fair game to attack anyone for no reason and never have to face the consequences (well, unless you troll Deontay Wilder, be careful).

We've all fallen prey to a troll to begin with because in the real world we give people the benefit of the doubt. But this doesn't apply online. We suffer from anxiety and stress resulting from troll attacks, as we unnecessarily try to explain ourselves to these basement-dwelling creatures (not to mention Cheetos smeared all over their face). Majority of troll interactions go south fast. This enhances our anxiety and stress.

The obvious way to counter this is just to disengage from trolls. This might be easier said than done, but it is the only sane solution. Would you try to reason with a person in the street yelling and abusing everybody? Of course not, so why try and reason with a troll who is the digital version of the crazy person in the street. It is much healthier for you to not engage with trolls. You won't be anxious or stressed. And if they are vicious and don't go away, just block them. But in most cases, they will go away if you don't fuel their fire.

You have to be strong and not feel the need to defend yourself. The troll doesn't really know you so why defend yourself to a crazy person? You need to keep that in mind before you respond to a troll's nonsense. You can turn this into a meditation practice. If someone writes a ridiculous comment on your YouTube video or Facebook post, just let it sit there and starve it of oxygen or delete it if needed. Why respond to bullshit? A troll is fishing for your reaction, but if your online presence is a fishless lake they will move onto other waters.

Let your intuition sense where there is trouble ahead. If you sense that a comment has the potential to go south if you engage then just leave it, it's not life or death. The amount of time this will free up for you is extraordinary. People wonder why many creative people get a lot done. If you view their social media network, they are not monitoring it by the minute. They post and logout, the rest will take care of itself. You should be the same. Post and logout. If no one hits the like button, then who really cares. Life is not a popularity contest. Waiting for people to respond and then defending yourself against trolls is just time wasting and illustrates that on a subtle level you are attracted to drama just like the troll.

If you wish to be healthy, sane, and ultimately peaceful, you need to eliminate drama from your life and your attraction to drama. This is not only important for how we deal with trolls but also for how we mindlessly consume the world's drama through the news.

Don't Watch the News

I've heard people make the excuse that they're checking their phone all the time to stay up to date on the news. They remind me of George Costanza in *Seinfeld* when he explained to Kramer that his meaning for getting up in the morning in his sad life is to get the daily news. In a way, we are all unconsciously trained to keep up with the current news. We are all under the belief that we should know about everything going on, every day. But this is a relatively new phenomenon. It's only existed since the advent of the television and radio that we even had access to what is going on around the world.

So, for hundreds of thousands of years we never had the news and guess what, we survived without it. In the 13th century while Genghis Khan was conquering Eurasia, the Native Americans were none the wiser of his conquest, nor did it matter to them because they didn't know about it. Was it the Native Americans' responsibility to know about such current events? Of course not. These sorts of events have occurred on this planet all throughout recorded history, and unless we become mature, they will continue to happen. Just like the Native Americans, you have no responsibility to stay up to date with the news.

We've developed this weird attitude that we should all know the current news because this shows we care. This is nonsense. I've been on the end of this ridiculous attitude because I never watch the news. Some ignorant people believe this type of action demonstrates that I don't care. Actually, it's quite the opposite considering I don't consume daily news as entertainment, which is really what it has become. I still hear about the news. But it's in the same way that Zen master Thich Nhat Hanh explained to Oprah Winfrey that if it is something truly important then he will hear about it. This is the same for myself.

If it's something important like the devastating floods in Pakistan back in 2010 or the coronavirus outbreak, then I will hear about it down the grapevine. You don't need to watch the news to hear about real *important* news. And I really don't hear about much news. You know why? Because 99% of news is not really important. The news networks are like any TV show or media outlet, they have to have content no matter if it is a really slow news day. It doesn't matter if the news is important or not.

What people don't consider is daily there is not that much stuff happening in the world to fill a thirty-minute or one-hour timeslot. There are some days in the world where nothing extreme happens. Usually on these days they'll follow up a news story from previous days, hopefully so they can rehash it day after day to its nth degree. Or they'll run a ridiculous story of two dogs getting married wearing little doggie wedding clothes. Very important stuff (sarcasm). If 99% of the news is not truly important then if you're a consumer of the news every day you waste 99% of your time viewing the news.

If the majority of the news has no real impact on your life then what are you consuming and how is it affecting you? The news networks are in the business of spoon-feeding you drama. And drama is never usually positive news but rather negative. The news networks either intelligently or unconsciously feed our negativity bias which keeps a lot of people locked into a state of fear. There is no real threat out there like a lion chasing us down on the Savanna in Africa, but the news tells us there is a threat somewhere and you should worry.

A news watcher's fight-or-flight response is subtly turned up, keeping them on guard from the "threat." Considering the majority of people view the news through numerous digital devices means most of the world is walking around in fear of some "threat" the news told them about. This is not a healthy state of mind, especially considering there is no real threat out there the majority of the time.

The news networks feed our negativity bias which in turn fuels our penchant for drama. This has intensified as our online activity has increased. We actively go looking for the news online to stay up to date by the minute. We are in the bad habit of seeking drama to fill our boredom. This is why gossip is so valuable to the media. If you are entertained by gossip you should feel shame, because what right do you have to know about people's private lives and have an opinion on their lives. Our attraction to gossip and negative news proves our psychologically unhealthy addiction to drama. The news could help the world out with not feeding us more negative drama, but they are in the business of ratings and how popular an article is online.

In a sane world, positive news should be the focus of the news media and there are many wonderful things happening in this world every day, but we just don't hear about it. Actually, there is a lot more positive news going on in the world than negative. But you won't hear about it nor may you be interested in it because you're addicted to drama. The online world magnifies your addiction. But if you want to be a healthy and sane individual you have to stop watching or reading the news. This has a twofold effect: first it will begin to cure your addiction to drama making you more positive in return, and secondly this act will help you reduce your online activity because you've ceased searching for the latest piece of news or drama to entertain you.

Staying up to date with the news doesn't help you one bit. People believe it's weird not to be up to speed on current events, but it's truly weird to know everything that is going on in the world. A world that believes we should know everything happening in the daily news is ignorant. You will never do or create anything meaningful with your life if your negativity and fear are constantly spiked by the daily concerns peddled by the media. Staying up to date with the news is actually harming you and stunts your conscious growth.

You need to stay away from the news not only online but also through other digital mediums and traditional forms such as TV, radio, and newspaper. If someone asks you about a current event and you don't know about it then that's fine. You don't have to feel guilty because you don't know what is happening in the world. Actually, news consumers don't really know what is going on in the world other than a version of it that the news wants to portray. Often a negative portrait. There is a lot of misinformation spread by the news which you have to consider before taking it as gospel (a whole other conversation).

Besides all this, you have no obligation to know what's happening in the world. It doesn't mean you don't care, but rather that you've begun to take control of your life and are starting to care for your mind. Life goes on with or without you, so choosing health and sanity requires you to stay away from worldly drama. I remember how many world events ticked off my dad and he's dead now, so it seems like such a waste of time and energy. The news is going on without my dad and it is likewise with you as well. It's really up to you to choose your own health and sanity over the insanity the news breeds. This simple method will allow you to be more positive and able to live a healthier and more productive lifestyle, offline. These methods for reducing online activity are helped along by an offline lifestyle that brings us back in contact with the real world and it is an expert approach to reach the best version of yourself.

Offline Lifestyle to Cure Online Addiction

To cure ourselves of our dependency and addiction to digital technology requires us to slow down and simplify our lives. Some rare people can identify something that is not benefiting their lives and begin to reduce or stop it altogether. Most of us don't fall into that category. Many of us need discipline to transform certain habits. This also goes for our attraction to the digital world. Actually, we've become such an undisciplined world, allowing our mind to run here and there while we achieve nothing other than wasting a lot of time in unconscious mode.

Rather than tending to our social media persona, we need to develop an offline lifestyle that takes care of human technology. Luckily, I have developed that system for you. In my book *Emotional Intuition for Peak Performance* I lay out the peak performance formula, which is based on the four fundamentals of human life: meditation, nutrition, exercise, and sleep. We often neglect the four fundamentals with our super busy lives, of which the digital world is a large contributor.

The four fundamentals enhance our life because we discipline our life, which allows us to reach our optimal potential. The four fundamentals reorient our focus from all the busyness and glitz and glamour of our lives to the pure simplicity that allows us to live life in the first place. Nourishing the four fundamentals is about taking care of the simple things. What most people don't understand is that by nourishing the simple things in our lives we are more productive and mentally stable.

Nourishing the four fundamentals enhances our ability to cultivate intelligence, harness creativity, and experience equanimity. You can't access any of these at a deep level if you are constantly busy. You might be able to produce something, but it won't be at a profound level. Taking tender care of the four fundamentals is an expert discipline that will weed out the distractions that don't serve you, such as digital devices. Let's examine the four fundamentals.

Meditation

Meditation is a no-brainer, literally. Only in recent times has meditation had widespread appeal because we are in desperate need of mind management in our over busy lives. But meditation not only manages the mind; it has far deeper implications. Meditation will, if practiced constantly for long enough, blunt your emotional responses, making you more conscious of your spontaneous thoughts, feelings, and emotions. This ability to catch our emotions is significantly weakened when we are too busy and tired. If we don't get enough sleep it is more difficult to be aware of our reactions. Meditation will help this problem, but it is more effective if we have sufficient sleep (something I'll discuss later in this chapter). If you do get sufficient sleep meditation can work its magic more powerfully.

In blunting our spontaneous reactions and urges we will begin to cease reaching unconsciously for our phone or checking our social media and e-mail every five minutes. You will become more conscious of your unconscious habits and tendencies. This is only positive for your life. You will stop wasting time fidgeting with your phone or surfing the Web unconsciously. Not only will meditation achieve this result, but it will also make you more efficient and ironically less busy and agitated in your mind.

This process puts you on a path to experience your natural bliss which I mentioned last chapter. The reason why bliss begins to arise ever so slowly is because in the act of sitting meditation your prefrontal cortex is temporarily disengaged if you are meditating properly.

Disengaging the prefrontal cortex every day will train your mind to stop overthinking. Your mind will be less agitated as your prefrontal cortex is not hyper-analyzing everything. Your mind will be far more stable and present, with a clear view of the spontaneous emotions that arise. You could say that your prefrontal cortex is more present rather than off in the future analyzing the life in front of you. And not being constantly in your head (PFC) allows the stuck fight-or-flight switch of the sympathetic nervous system to be turned off.

This leads to another reason why bliss is experienced: we are accessing the parasympathetic nervous system. The more we meditate the more we access the parasympathetic nervous system. Accessing the parasympathetic nervous system daily trains us to be calmer in the storm of life. Life and its obstacles don't bother you as much. This is the benefit of accessing the parasympathetic nervous system daily through meditation. Your nervous system will not be tuned tightly, allowing your life and mind to be more effortless.

These two reasons are why bliss arises from within you. But you have to make sure you are meditating properly. There are a lot of fake meditation techniques out there that are not grounded in tradition nor have thousands of years of practice and research to back them up. New-age meditation techniques and the warping of traditional techniques are not grounded and based on thousands of years of experiential knowledge and are basically designed to turn meditation into a commodity.

The meditation practices I have been involved with and teach are more traditional and effective. I've learned these from living in Asia and learning these techniques from various Eastern traditions. These meditation methods are sitting meditative techniques because they are designed to work on the mind level directly. Working on the mind level directly impacts your habits and tendencies which ultimately transforms your actions.

The most beneficial tools to work on the deep mind level are the breath and also placing our attention on our mental activity. The first method I recommend is *vipassana*. Vipassana is a Pali word that means "insight into your true nature" or it is simply translated as "insight meditation." Vipassana is believed to be the original teaching of the Buddha. This technique has been turned into a ten-day retreat program where you practice vipassana meditation for ten hours a day totaling one hundred hours in ten days. Now a ten-day course will transform your life, but constant daily vipassana has far greater implications if you can maintain the practice. The reason it is so effective is because vipassana is really a science designed to get down to the sensory level of our psychosomatic organism.

Vipassana is essentially a science for transforming the subconscious, which is important considering our negative habits and tendencies. The sensory level is believed to be where we transform our subconscious because its impulses are at the root of the mind-body matrix, and the impulses at the root level are those unconscious sensations. This transformation is achieved by using the breath as our anchor (anchor is a word commonly used in meditation that refers to a place we put our awareness in the process of meditation). This anchor in vipassana is known in Pali as *anapanasati*, which means "awareness of respiration."

Observing the breath may seem simple, but it's not. The difficulty with the vipassana technique of anapanasati is we are taught to place our awareness on our breathing without altering its natural rhythm. Essentially, you want to just watch your breath without changing its rhythm. But the problem is you will change its rhythm when you begin to think about what you're doing. It does take time to master this skill, but when you do it is super effective for bringing equanimity to your mind.

Another expert meditation technique is found in Zen Buddhism. This technique is commonly known as "open-awareness meditation." This method is more about awareness than breathing. Open-awareness meditation is focused on becoming conscious of mental activity. We place our awareness on the stream of consciousness, which are all the thoughts that continuously bubble up in our mind, including all the stories we tell ourselves. Zen master Thich Nhat Hanh says that when we are unconscious of the stream of consciousness, we are like cows ruminating on food, but the food human beings are ruminating on are thoughts. In open-awareness meditation it is an interesting discovery to see that when we observe our thoughts they disappear like a ghost. We put into jeopardy the validity of some of the thoughts we have rattling around inside our skull the more we practice open-awareness meditation. As a result, from consistent discipline our inner landscape begins to become more tranquil, where the waves of thoughts begin to cease movement and our mind becomes as transparent and reflective as an undisturbed lake.

With both practices, you will notice how the mind has a tendency to wander, which takes your awareness away from its anchor. The goal for any serious meditator is to shorten those periods of mind wandering. The more you practice either method, the shorter these mind wandering periods will be. The most important thing is to notice that your mind is wandering and bring your awareness back to its anchor, otherwise you could drift off for several minutes. This has to be your primary meditative exercise.

Both of these techniques should be first practiced for twenty minutes in the morning and before bed at night. But to get more benefits you need to increase your time sitting to thirty minutes and if you want to go monk mode then forty-five minutes to an hour is optimal.

Nutrition

Nutrition may seem unrelated to our dependency and addiction to digital technology, but this is an oversight. What we eat and drink on a daily basis can either fuel our agitated mind to play mindlessly with digital devices or the act of playing with digital devices develops bad eating habits. This is an argument to what comes first, the chicken or the egg? But this argument doesn't really matter because both views are right. Either way you look at it, they both lead to bad health if we are not conscious of what we are eating and also how we childishly play with digital devices.

Nevertheless, people discount how what we eat contributes to our dependency and addiction to living in the artificial digital world. Our food choices are critical in our fight to reclaim our natural life from the clutches of digital tyranny. What you eat and drink determines how agitated your mind is. An agitated mind can't sit still and needs constant stimulation, which is usually appeased by digital technology. We have to uproot the food choices that agitate the mind. We live in a world of excess and our eating habits reflect this greed. We are a generation of overeaters and overeating itself will agitate the mind. But especially the food we choose to overeat with.

Our modern diets are built on fillers. These fillers are usually heavy carbs such as bread, rice, and starchy vegetables. We've all bought into the idea that a high-carb low-fat diet is the healthiest for us. But our growing waistline and increase in diseases tells another story. The accepted notion that fat is bad and carbs are great has to be reevaluated and thankfully it has in modern science. Sure, there are certain fats that are not the best, such as trans-fat. But healthy fat in general is not what makes us overweight, and unhealthy, excessive carbohydrates do. People gorge through loaves of bread and bowls of rice and wonder why their waistlines are expanding. "I don't eat fried food like French fries," they say, and that is great but then you see them eat a footlong sandwich as if all that wheat is supposed to be good for us. Well it isn't. The flabbiness and puffy skin rolls so common in the modern body shape are the result of an excessive carb-centered diet.

We all know the culprit for an unattractive beer belly. But we don't want to look at the elephant in the room in regards to obesity, grains especially wheat. Our habit of eating excessive wheat, rice, and grains in general, is terrible for us. For example, wheat, especially the refined variety, enhances our chances of disease, obesity, and affects brain health. If you want an optimal state of mind then excessive grains should be avoided. One of the main reasons is gluten. Gluten is a mixture of proteins found in wheat and other related grains. It is something we should avoid at all costs if we want a healthy brain and tranquil mind. But if you go gluten-free you must eat enough dietary fiber from gluten-free fiber containing grains. However, fiber doesn't have to come just from grain as it can also be found in foods rich in prebiotic fiber such as jicama, onion, garlic, chicory root, dandelion root, and Jerusalem artichoke, to name just a few. Neurologist Dr. David Perlmutter explains the health issues concerning gluten and the brain:

> Gluten is a foreign protein to human physiology, and is the cornerstone of leaky brain—causing inflammation. Science has made some amazing discoveries about the blood brain barrier in recent years, most importantly that it can become just as permeable as our gut lining. When gluten is introduced to the body, it turns out that inflammation [is what] degrades this important barrier.[1]

Along with fillers in our modern diet is our overconsumption and consequential addiction to sugar (sugar is a carbohydrate). People are unknowingly addicted to sugar. Sugar, especially refined fructose, is almost in everything in the supermarket. It is in a lot of our food and drinks, anywhere from pasta sauce to baby food and milk. The sugar in a lot of processed foods and drinks is usually fructose which occurs in inert sugar, honey, and a great many fruits. But this is not a beat-up on fruit; fruit is healthy for you in moderation. But if you are consuming a few mangoes and some dried fruit a day, for example, then that is far too much sugar intake. Fruits, such as blueberries and avocados, are low-sugar and full of nutrition.

We are unknowingly addicted to sugar. Every day on average people exceed their daily sugar consumption. Someone will have a burger meal and wash it down with Coca-Cola and think it was great until that low depressive feeling comes along from too much sugar (in fast-food burgers and basically any poor-quality food sugar is found). Excessive sugar will mess with your mind and overstimulate your nervous system. Both excessive grains and sugar lead to numerous psychological problems and nervous system diseases (gluten and excessive sugar consumption are both instrumental in the development of Alzheimer's disease).

Overstimulating the gut with heavy carbs and sugar affects the stability of the mind. Carbs spike our insulin leading to agitation and irritation. When this agitation affects the mind we can't sit still and so we play irrationally with our digital devices. On top of both carbs and sugar is spicy food. Eating overly spicy food will cause too much heat in your body and, as result, agitate your mind. Chili specifically is the main culprit. Not only will overly spicy food agitate your mind leading to mindlessly engaging in the digital world, but it will also disturb your sleep.

Last, but definitely not least regarding nutrition, is how

much caffeine we consume, especially through coffee. We've become addicted to the irritable high that comes from caffeine (it is a psychoactive after all). Our coffee culture is addicted to that feeling which really is borderline ADHD (attention deficit hyperactivity disorder). The speed and intensity caffeine has on our mind is evident in the speech and actions of those high on it. With the growing trend of cafés on every corner many people are becoming addicted. For someone who doesn't drink coffee, I find it increasingly difficult to converse with people high on caffeine because their mind is so agitated that they replicate a fidgety kid with ADHD.

Coffee depletes our nervous system which in turn contributes to anxiety and psychological problems such as panic attacks and depression. A lot of people believe coffee helps them focus. But though you may be sharp and alert, you have no real clarity because the mind is going off like lights on a Christmas tree. Excessive caffeine agitates our mind and compels us to act. We often burn out or feel low after coming off a caffeine high. The problem is many people just refuel when they are lacking energy and continue to push the limits without realizing they are draining their energy systems while causing long-term damage. Sleep is another aspect of our life that caffeine disrupts. Every waking minute a chemical called adenosine is building up in your brain. The buildup of adenosine in the brain increases our desire to sleep. This is known as sleep pressure. Adenosine is artificially muted when we ingest caffeine. Caffeine essentially blocks adenosine, acting as a masking agent. Nevertheless, adenosine continues to build up. Once your liver dismantles caffeine from your system all of the adenosine that has been silently building up comes flooding back into your system like a dam that has had its walls burst. This phenomenon is commonly known as a "caffeine crash." But you may argue that you drink your coffee (or your last coffee) in the late morning or early afternoon and so it doesn't affect you. It is true that levels of caffeine circulating in our body peak thirty minutes after drinking. But the problem is caffeine is very persistent, which is an oversight by many people. In pharmacology, they use the term "half-life" for a drug's efficacy. Half-life simply refers to the length of time it takes for the body to remove fifty percent of a drug's concentration. The average half-life of caffeine is five to seven hours. So, sneaking in an afternoon coffee has the potential to disrupt your sleep many hours later. This is the harmful effects of caffeine on our sleep.

For these reasons, and many more, coffee is considered to have little, if any, value as a food in traditional Chinese medicine (TCM). The science in TCM explains that coffee produces too much yang (heat) in the body, causing the body to be out of balance with yin (coolant). Too much heat is produced by certain foods such as coffee. As a result, being too active and thinking too much are both by-products of coffee. Chinese medical doctor Brendan Kelly explains the effects of coffee:

> For many of us, drinking coffee can produce a long list of symptoms... and can contribute to, or create, a wide range of [others], including anxiety, racing thoughts, insomnia, disturbed dreams, headaches (including migraines), acid reflux, irritable bowel syndrome, a wide range of stomach and intestinal issues, fibroids of all kinds (including uterine fibroids), growths of all kinds (including tumors), a wide range of skin conditions including eczema, arthritis, a wide range of pain conditions (including fibromyalgia), heart palpitations, excess anger and aggression, dizziness and vertigo, lower-back and leg weakness and pain, a lack of rooted energy in general. In fact, all chronic and acute conditions that involve heat from the Chinese perspective and inflammation from the Western perspective are likely exacerbated by coffee.[2]

This irritability caused by caffeine transfers over into bad digital habits, such as scrolling mindlessly through social media feeds. A calm mind will not seek out such stimulation. A healthy alternative to coffee is tea, especially noncaffeinated tea. I personally consume master herbalist Ron Teeguarden's Spring Dragon Longevity Tea in the morning, usually while I write as I am doing right now writing these words. This tea contains no caffeine. Other teas to consider are green tea, oolong tea, and pu'er tea. Green tea has a small quantity of caffeine which adds more to its calming effect. But be mindful how much caffeine all tea has, as some green tea, oolong tea, and pu'er tea can also be loaded with caffeine. Good tea tends to be soothing and evokes creativity. But beware if they are too loaded in caffeine.

Identifying the effects of heavy carbs, sugar, and caffeine will help stabilize your mind if you choose a healthy diet. An increase in healthy fats and a decrease in carbs, sugar, and caffeine is essential for optimal health. A low-carb high quality fat lifestyle leads to greater clarity and a sharpened ability to focus, both of which are missing in a high-carb low-fat diet because this outdated diet continues to make us sluggish and fall into the distraction of digital technology. Instead of eating a salad sandwich, just eat salad. Fall in love with vegetables and healthy fats. As for coffee, giving it away altogether is the best for your mind and your digital addiction. Choose a noncaffeinated tea and cultivate tranquility and peace in your life. And last, but not least, stay away from junk food and processed food, as both usually have a lethal combination of carbs, sugar, and caffeine. Be conscious of your nutritional choices and watch your attraction for digital stimulation decrease.

Exercise

Daily exercise is something most of us don't do. Especially in the digital age. The digital human is predominately sedentary. We'll sit for hours in front of a digital screen and not move our bodies. This habit keeps us locked in the mind and not in the body. I know this best being a writer. If I sit and write for too long, I feel exhausted because it feels like I've run a marathon, and I probably have along the neural pathways of my brain.

A daily exercise routine keeps me in my body. This is especially beneficial if I keep a strict time-block for writing of between three and four hours, usually in the morning. Exercise is for everybody though, not just anxious writers. A sedentary lifestyle is relatively new, born from jobs that ask us to sit for hours at work and also our computer and TV lifestyles. We are naturally designed to move and we are supposed to move a lot of time each day. Our ancestors moved a lot more than we do today and they didn't have half the physical and psychological problems we have.

Many people who suffer from diseases such as depression, obesity, chronic anxiety, etc., usually don't move a lot and are commonly lazy. Sitting around all the time doesn't turn on certain chemicals in our brain that help nourish an optimal state. Aerobic exercise actually changes our gene expression. Research explains that this has something to do with certain chemicals in our brain that are turned on during exercise. Increased levels of a crucial protein called brain-derived neurotrophic factor (BDNF) are produced during exercise. BDNF allows our brain cells to communicate with each other in a far more efficient manner. This leads to a settled mind with clarity, the mind's response to feeling optimal health and well-being. The great feeling we have after exercise is due to BDNF being turned on.

This settled mind can be experienced with just twenty minutes of aerobic exercise a day. Obviously, you can increase your intensity as you gain fitness, but it is remarkable how just twenty minutes can lead to a stable mind. Moving the body through intense exercise will get you out of your head and back into the body. This brings more clarity and an awareness of the ill health our digital lives have produced. Reduce your online sitting activity and increase your natural movement activity.

Sleep

Sleep hygiene is a common term used now in regards to protecting ourselves in ways that guarantee a good night sleep. This term has come about due to the bombardment of digital technology and our busy lives, which both deprive us of healthy sleep. But even though we all want to sleep better and deeper, most people don't know how to guarantee it.

The way we achieve more consistent sleep patterns is by making sleep a priority. Actually, it should be the number one priority in the four fundamentals because the other three fundamentals suffer if we don't get enough sleep. We will be too tired to have consistent exercise, our diets will fall back into bad habits because with less sleep our decision-making ability is decreased and we usually gravitate towards unhealthy food, and lastly our meditation won't be deep because our mind is naturally agitated with less sleep and also because it is likely that if you're not getting enough sleep then you are a busy person and busyness molds our mind into the habit of being whisked around like scrambled eggs. A busy mind lives in the shallows and can never go deep. But if we want to live deep and meaningful lives then we have to prioritize our sleep.

Sleeping preferably eight hours a day is optimal (it's considered healthy to sleep between seven to nine hours a day). Consistently sleeping for this duration every day allows the natural function of non-rapid eye movement sleep (NREM) and rapid-eye movement sleep (REM) to fluctuate naturally, nourishing our entire being. As a result, we consolidate important memories better, we enhance our learning ability, we are more creative and productive, we aren't emotional and have a sense of calm, and last but not least we have a mind that is equanimous rather than agitated. The well-rested, as a result, usually have very meaningful lives. But that is available to all of us. It's like a magical medicine we all have access to. Scientist and professor of neuroscience and psychology at the University of California, Berkeley, Matthew Walker explains this magical medicine with good humor:

> Scientists have discovered a revolutionary new treatment that makes you live longer. It enhances your memory and makes you more creative. It makes you look more attractive. It keeps you slim and lowers food cravings. It protects you from cancer and dementia. It wards off colds and the flu. It lowers your risk of heart attacks and stroke, not to mention diabetes. You'll even feel happier, less depressed, and less anxious. Are you interested?[3]

All of these health benefits sleep provides are diminished with the use of digital technology. The digital world agitates our mind which directly pushes back on sleep. Our mind's constant engagement with this digital world is literally killing our mind, as we coexist in a suboptimal state. The constant engagement is especially unhealthy at nighttime.

Many people are in the habit of using digital devices any spare moment they have, especially at night. At night people want to chill out by watching television, surfing the Internet on either a computer, laptop, tablet, or phone, and basically people play with their phone all night. Though we may feel chilled out, we are not truly relaxing. We are really relaxing when we cease activity. Stimulating our mind through the input we take in via the eyes and ears is still activity, as we are stimulating the sympathetic nervous system. The mind is being agitated by sensory input. To truly relax means to stop a lot of sensory input and allow the mind to just settle in this present moment.

Using digital devices at night stimulates the sympathetic nervous system too much, leading to disorders such as insomnia. Actually, research explains that one of the main contributors to insomnia and restless nights is from the blue light in digital devices.

We've all experienced a restless night's sleep after we had stared at our phone, television, laptop, etc., just before bed. Some of us have evolved to stare at our phones in bed. The scientific research of blue light's effect on our mind reveals a connection between bad sleep patterns and digital devices. The blue light in digital devices depletes our pineal gland, a pea-sized organ in the brain. The pineal gland is a primary organ for facilitating a good deep sleep. A few hours before our regular bedtime the pineal gland begins to release melatonin (a hormone produced in the pineal gland that regulates biological rhythms) which reduces your alertness and makes sleep more inviting. But blue light stops the pineal gland from releasing melatonin and so we remain alert and ready for action as if it is daytime. Exposure to blue light, or LED light in general, at nighttime stops the pineal gland from secreting melatonin and ultimately messes with our circadian rhythms, affecting our sleep patterns.[a]

This is the science of what digital devices are doing to your sleep and ultimately your health. So, before you clutch at your phone in bed getting that last tweet away, think again before this unconscious action. Actually, the first method to prioritize sleep is to have no digital devices in the bedroom. There can be no excuses, such as using it for an alarm clock. As I mentioned, invest in a traditional alarm clock, this will help your sleep rather than being enticed by your phone. Keep your sleeping space digi-free. But to truly counter the blue light problem, prioritizing sleep begins much earlier in the evening.

One such method is *digital sunsets*. The phrase digital sunset was coined by philosopher and optimal life coach Brian Johnson. Digital sunsets consist of shutting down all digital devices, including turning off your phone, by at least 6pm, preferably 5pm for maximum benefits. The next time you turn on your digital devices is when you begin your workday the following day, not before that.

Cal Newport applies this approach to his life. At 5pm every day after addressing all his e-mails and other matters he shuts his computer down and finishes the workday by stating "shutdown complete." This end of workday mantra symbolizes that he has truly finished his work for the day and won't see another digital screen until the following workday. The digital sunset approach allows him to be more present with his family at night.

Digital sunsets allow us the time to enjoy each other's company again, without the interference of a digital device. Talking face to face is far better than chatting on social media. Digital sunsets address the blue light issue. It is a great method for curing insomnia and correcting poor sleep patterns. Digital sunsets enhance melatonin production and as a result enhance health and well-being.

Deep sleep is guaranteed if you practice digital sunsets. This will also curb your addiction to online activity and mindlessly fidgeting with your phone. The peak performance formula of the four fundamentals is an offline lifestyle that helps cure our digital dependency and addiction. Keeping our ordinary life simple through nourishing the four fundamentals helps our mind remain stable without an urge for stimulation. This will not magically happen for you. It requires a complete makeover of your life and a commitment to spending most of your day in real life rather than in front of a screen. This way of life requires us to return to a mindset pre-digital age.

Note

a. For more on the relationship between sleep, the pineal gland, and blue light see the following articles: "The Role of Melatonin in the Circadian Rhythm Sleep-Wake Cycle," by Atul Khullar, www.psychiatrictimes.com/view/role-melatonin-circadian-rhythm-sleep-wake-cycle; "Blue light has a dark side," from

Harvard Health Publications, www.health.harvard.edu/ staying-healthy/blue-light-has-a-dark-side; and "Seeing Blue: The Impact of Excessive Blue Light Exposure," by Heather Flint Ford, www.reviewofoptometry.com/article/seeing-blue-the-impact-of-excessive-blue-light-exposure.

Chapter 10

Return to the Ancient Way of Life

Pre-digital age might seem a long time ago, but it was just yesterday. We have only really felt the impact of digital technology in the last ten years, not even a blink of the eye of evolution. Life before digital technology and the Internet appears ancient. But even as young as I am (38 writing this book) I was born before both and I remember how wonderful life was back then (now I'm starting to sound like my dad).

Call me old fashioned, but human life was much more vivid back then. People spoke face to face, we weren't bombarded by the advertising industry, and the world wasn't saturated with information. These are only a few examples. But life can still be this way, though it does require our commitment to living a healthy lifestyle. This lifestyle is committed to simplifying our lives and reducing digital technology's impact on our lives.

Simple Living Minus Digital Technology

To live in a healthy and sane world we have to examine digital technology's impact on our immediate lives. To put everything you've learned in this book into action you need to be brutally honest and radical when examining your technological use. You want to turn your life into a "classic," in the same way that many of us appreciate the beauty and craftsmanship of a classic car. Our life has to be a classic, in the sense of living a life that is simple and geared towards a way of life pre-digital age.

Living simply means we must claim our attention back from digital technology. Everything that distorts our attention must be reduced or eradicated. First of all, there is no need to have all the digital devices such as a smartphone, tablet, laptop, and desktop computer. Unless you are in some specialized field, there is no need for all of these devices. If you want a home computer buy either a laptop or desktop, but not both. As for a portable device, you don't need both a phone and tablet. Choose which one is practical for your life but not both.

Obviously using any of these devices should be minimal. Use them for what you specifically need them for, but don't let your attention wander down the rabbit hole of the digital world. In fact, when moving around, such as walking, keep the phone always in your pocket or bag. As I mentioned earlier, nothing is that important that you have to stare at the screen as you walk.

Another bad habit has also occurred from owning smartphones, and that is people have ear devices plugged into their ears always listening to something other than what is going on around them. This is disastrous for our attention. I remember trekking with my wife in the Himalayas for eighteen days. One day we were walking and I was in my head distracted by my thoughts and not conscious of the world around me (a common unconscious state for the mind to be in). My wife then commented on the beautiful sound of the cicadas in chorus as we walked. Only then did I realize that I was tuned into Radio Non-Stop Thinking (Radio NST), as Thich Nhat Hanh puts it. After her comment I was tuned into reality going on around me, a beautiful calming state always available. The big problem for the modern individual is they are tuned into both Radio NST and also whatever they are listening to through their ear devices. Our attention is completely fragmented as a result.

It's astonishing the number of people who walk around with ear devices plugged in. It's become the craze, where Bluetooth headphones are simple because they're cordless and connect with a smartphone (some ear devices look like bulky ear safety headphones you find on construction sites). Though people think this is cool and important to stay up to speed with the new trends, what is really happening is they are subtly asleep. When I see people with these ear devices on, I recognize a person not really in the moment. I recognize an unconscious individual. And yes, if you do wear these audio devices while actively doing something else such as walking then you are unconscious because your attention is fragmented and out of sync with the immediate environment.

These audio devices lock us into our head and fuel Radio NST. And I mean all audio devices, cordless and cords. Not to mention the new cordless Bluetooth ear buds that look like earrings which people somehow think is cool. Newsflash, they are not cool, they look ridiculous, but we all want them to keep up with the trends.

To simplify your life and reclaim your mind you need to say no to using ear devices when you are walking around or any other activity like running, etc., essentially doing something else. Our mind was not designed for multitasking, even though it is capable of multitasking. When we multitask, we over activate the sympathetic nervous system making us subtly anxious as we deplete our energy reserves.

When we are getting from A to B with our ear devices playing audio in our ears we are multitasking and causing subtle anxiety. To be healthy and sane we have to leave the ear devices at home. The truth is you are only listening to half of whatever is playing because you have to pay some attention to the immediate environment. It's better to engage in whatever it is you are listening to at home, where you can give your undivided attention which is beneficial. Giving yourself fully to one task is far more effective than trying to achieve multiple tasks.

Simplifying your life requires a dedication to not complexify it. The less digital input the better. Where you can reduce your technological use, you must. Lightening the load is important. Also choosing older forms of technology is positive. I mentioned last chapter about investing in a traditional alarm clock as opposed to using your smartphone. Having no digital technology in the bedroom is essential. And thankfully there are companies such as Punkt. (with a full-stop) who are conscious of the damage digital technology is having on the world. Punkt. is a Swiss consumer electronics company founded by entrepreneur Petter Neby. Neby's focus is on people living less distracted lives, as he explains:

Today's world is consumed with technology and I think we are too distracted by it in day-to-day life. I founded Punkt. to offer a viable alternative for those feeling overwhelmed by the advanced technologies that have pervaded modern lifestyles. Punkt. is about using technology to help us adopt good habits for less distracted lives.[1]

Punkt. is dedicated to a technological return to retro. And it is not their alarm clock that is making waves, but rather their slick push button phone that only texts and calls with no digital smartphone display screen. This is a very professional device and for anyone who is serious about living a healthy and sane life. It is amazing how a retro phone like Punkt. drastically decreases our unconscious fidgeting with a phone. First of all, the digital world does not reside in the Punkt. phone. This goes to show that it is not entirely the smartphone itself that is the problem, but rather our attraction to this relatively new artificial digital world. And the common attitude is that keeping up with the trends in the digital world is more important than a return to retro to reclaim our sanity.

Don't Keep Up with the Joneses or Entrepreneurs

Everybody is trying to keep up with each other when it comes to digital trends. You should see the look on people's faces when I explain that I don't know what WhatsApp is. I'm not sure why this is important, but people feel concerned for me. I've never been one to keep up with the Joneses because there is inherent delusion in trying to keep up with other people according to what people agree is important, such as having a mortgage, cars, kids, etc. But most people fall into the trap of keeping up with the Joneses and this translates over to digital technology.

Everybody wants the newest gadget because someone else has it and they won't feel left behind with people like myself. The idea that we need the latest gizmo to keep up with the Joneses is just plain idiotic and insecure. Are you not a sovereign individual who can think for yourself? It doesn't seem many people are and it is only getting worse. Digital culture is driving this hysteria.

At the coalface are numerous successful entrepreneurs who promote social media as a way of life and they themselves are none the wiser. Many entrepreneurs are constantly engaged in social media driving other people to do the same. Entrepreneurs often explain to their audience the so-called benefits of having a social media presence and being constantly engaged. These types of entrepreneurs become the template of success for most people. People try to replicate an entrepreneur but can't keep up with their level of social media presence. They don't realize an entrepreneur has a lot of people working for them. You can't have that level of activity on your own if you are creating work that matters.

Entrepreneurs clumsily promote this go-get-em-at-all-cost mentality which is focused only on doing. If you are doing, doing, doing, doing all the time then your sympathetic nervous system is overloaded and you are borderline insane. As a result, a lot of entrepreneurs are crazy people but they don't know it. The crazy entrepreneur is active all the time and, as a result, is slowly burning out and taking precious years off their life. Their audience follows suit and eventually burn out themselves chasing their own tails. Being successful is not worth dying for. Nor is it worth becoming crazy.

Being productive is important, but only if it is in balance

with doing nothing. Activating the sympathetic nervous system all the time leads to all sorts of psychological problems (as I mentioned earlier). Accessing the parasympathetic nervous system by doing nothing is cognitively healthy. Investing your entire life in a social media presence to attract attention and promote your sense of entrepreneurship is not healthy or sane. Entrepreneurs who advise people to seek Instagram followers, for example, to have a cool social media presence are doing a disservice to humanity. Don't listen to such entrepreneurs, they prey on your acquiescence.

We're always trying to keep up with each other as if it is important. As a result, we don't really live our lives because our lives become what others expect of us. We are always comparing our lives to others and social media fuels comparison. But comparison and keeping up with the Joneses leads to no form of happiness. As Theodore Roosevelt once said, "Comparison is the thief of joy." Your choice right now is to say no to that sort of attitude and reclaim who you truly are. Instead of doing what culture and society are driving you to be, have the balls (or ovaries) to live your life beyond the border of social convention.

Beyond the Border

Living beyond the border of what is considered "normal" is a commitment to the health and sanity of yourself and the world. Living beyond the border is about turning your life into a classic. You have an appreciation for the ancient ways, and design your life on their principles. My wife Gayoung often says that our relationship together is analog, and this is true not just for our relationship, but also for everybody. As I mentioned earlier, our minds are not designed for multitasking, but rather a one task at a time process.

Our minds, essentially, are analog not digital. Trying to make our minds operate like the digital world is killing us. We have to return to our analog nature. You have to appreciate the simple things. Living beyond the border of social convention means your life is on your terms and not influenced by social and cultural trends. Your motives are different. Essentially you have a completely different mindset from the masses. You'll naturally be attracted to deeper philosophies about life because beyond the border is where contemplation is enhanced. This leads to being more creative and inspired. Actually, all of the great sages and artists reside beyond the border.

From beyond the border you can look into the world objectively and see what is wrong and offer a solution. This objective view is especially important now because the digital world is killing us from the inside and so we need people who are a classic to lead by example and allow their health and sanity to be infectious. Becoming a classic person means you've reduced your digital devices and time spent on them, and invested in your attention which reaps the rewards of health and sanity.

A classic person is not interested in chasing their own tail like everybody else. Instead, beyond the border, by reducing or eliminating digital technology, you begin to taste that unassociated bliss that is all of our birthright. We have just never experienced it because getting a retweet on our latest tweet occupied all our mental bandwidth. Chasing your own tail trying to stand on the shoulders of others is not your true nature, it's a social attitude that you've borrowed.

Blissfulness is your true nature and you don't need anyone or anything to verify that because it just requires you to slow your life down and simplify it so your mind can finally become stable. We can all experience this but we have to have a commitment to everything in this book. We have to take our real life back and say no to the digital world always seeking our participation. You have to be fine with being different and learn to stand on your own two feet. You have to be fine with living your life rather than what the world wants you to be. You have to be fine with getting rid of your digital devices and reducing your digital interactions. You have to choose your own health and sanity if you want to live in a healthy and sane world. Finally, ask yourself, do you have the courage to travel beyond the border? Who knows, I might meet you there, where we can speak face to face as nature intended.

Notes

Chapter 1: The Evolution of Digital Culture and Robotic Behavior

1. Patrick Bet-David and Vanilla Ice, "Vanilla Ice Interview: Tupac, The 90's Generation & Selling 160 Million Records," *Valuetainment*, YouTube video posted February 22, 2018, https://www.youtube.com/watch?v=GOo0-7n3_tA

Chapter 4: The Psychology of the Digital Mind

1. Aja Romano, "Twitter released 9 million tweets from one Russian troll farm. Here's what we learned." Vox, https://www.vox.com/2018/10/19/17990946/twitter-russian-trolls-bots-election-tampering
2. Negativity Bias, https://en.wikipedia.org/wiki/Negativity_bias

Chapter 5: Rationality is Killing the Mind

1. Sherry Turkle, *Reclaiming Conversation*, rev. ed. (Penguin, 2016, 34). Turkle's appearance on *The Colbert Report* described in this cited passage from *Reclaiming Conversation* originally aired on January 17, 2011.
2. Sherry Turkle, *Reclaiming Conversation*, rev. ed. (Penguin, 2016, 35).
3. Sherry Turkle, *Reclaiming Conversation*, rev. ed. (Penguin, 2016, 3).

Chapter 7: Social Media Wants Your Soul

1. Tristan Harris, interview with Anderson Cooper, *60 Minutes*, https://www.cbsnews.com/news/brain-hacking-tech-insiders-60-minutes/
2. Bill Maher, "Social Media is the New Nicotine," *Real Time with Bill Maher*, YouTube video posted May 12, 2017, https://

www.youtube.com/watch?v=KDqoTDM7tio

3. Bill Maher, "Social Media is the New Nicotine," *Real Time with Bill Maher*, YouTube video posted May 12, 2017, https://www.youtube.com/watch?v=KDqoTDM7tio

4. Cal Newport, *Digital Minimalism* (Penguin, 2019, 17).

5. Mike Allen, "Sean Parker Unloads on Facebook: 'God only knows what it's doing to our children's brains,'" Axios, November 9, 2017, https://www.axios.com/sean-parker-unloads-on-facebook-god-only-knows-what-its-doing-to-our-childrens-brains-1513306792-f855e7b4-4e99-4d60-8d51-2775559c2671.html

6. Mike Allen, "Sean Parker Unloads on Facebook: 'God only knows what it's doing to our children's brains,'" Axios, November 9, 2017, https://www.axios.com/sean-parker-unloads-on-facebook-god-only-knows-what-its-doing-to-our-childrens-brains-1513306792-f855e7b4-4e99-4d60-8d51-2775559c2671.html

7. Jon E. Grant, Marc N. Potenza, Aviv Weinstein, and David A. Gorelick, "Introduction to Behavioral Addictions," *American Journal of Drug and Alcohol Abuse* 36, no. 5 (2010): 233-41, https://www.ncbi.nlm.nih.gov/pmc/articles/PMC3164585/

8. "Addiction," Substance Abuse, *Psychology Today*, https://www.psychologytoday.com/basics/addiction

9. Joe Rogan and Jonathan Haidt, "Social Media is Giving Kids Anxiety," YouTube video posted January 7, 2019, https://www.youtube.com/watch?v=CI6rX96oYnY

10. Joe Rogan and Jonathan Haidt, "Social Media is Giving Kids Anxiety," YouTube video posted January 7, 2019, https://www.youtube.com/watch?v=CI6rX96oYnY

11. Joe Rogan and Jonathan Haidt, "Social Media is Giving Kids Anxiety," YouTube video posted January 7, 2019, https://www.youtube.com/watch?v=CI6rX96oYnY

12. Joe Rogan and Jonathan Haidt, "Social Media is Giving Kids

Anxiety," YouTube video posted January 7, 2019, https://www.youtube.com/watch?v=CI6rX96oYnY

13. Joe Rogan and Jonathan Haidt, "Social Media is Giving Kids Anxiety," YouTube video posted January 7, 2019, https://www.youtube.com/watch?v=CI6rX96oYnY

14. Joe Rogan and Jonathan Haidt, "Social Media is Giving Kids Anxiety," YouTube video posted January 7, 2019, https://www.youtube.com/watch?v=CI6rX96oYnY

15. Sherry Turkle, *Reclaiming Conversation*, rev. ed. (Penguin, 2016, 158).

Chapter 9: A Digital-Free Lifestyle

1. Perlmutter, David. "How Can Eating Gluten Affect the Health of My Brain?" davidperlmutter MD, www.drperlmutter.com/can-eating-gluten-affect-health-brain/

2. Brendan Kelly, *The Yin and Yang of Climate Crisis* (North Atlantic Books, 2015, 54, 55).

3. Matthew Walker, *Why We Sleep* (Penguin, 2018, 107).

Chapter 10: Return to the Ancient Way of Life

1. Petter Neby, https://www.punkt.ch/en/about-punkt/history/

Bibliography

Agrawal, Ajay, Joshua Gans, and Avi Goldfarb. *Prediction Machines*. Boston, MA: Harvard Business Review Press, 2018.

Alter, Adam. *Irresistible*. New York: Penguin, 2017.

Austin, James. *Zen and the Brain*. Cambridge, MA: MIT Press, 1999.

Barrat, James. *Our Final Invention*. New York: Thomas Dunne Books, 2013.

Beilock, Sian. *Choke*. New York: Free Press, 2010.

Benoit, Hubert. *Zen and the Psychology of Transformation*. Rochester, VT: Inner Traditions, 1990.

Bostrom, Nick. *Superintelligence*. New York: Oxford University Press, 2016.

Campbell, Joseph. *Myths of Light*. Novato, CA: New World Library, 2003.

Campbell, Joseph. *Pathways to Bliss*. Novato, CA: New World Library, 2004.

Campbell, Joseph. *The Power of Myth*. New York: Anchor Books, 1991.

Chuang-tzu. *The Complete Works of Chuang Tzu*. Translated by Burton Watson. New York: Columbia University Press, 1968.

Clark, Andy. *Being There: Putting Brain, Body, and World Together Again*. Cambridge, MA: A Bradford Book, 1997.

Confucius. *Analects*. Translated by Edward Slingerland. Indianapolis, IN: Hackett Publishing, 2003.

Csikszentmihalyi, Mihaly. *Flow*. New York: Harper and Row, 1990.

Daugherty, Paul R., and H. James Wilson. *Human + Machine*. Boston, MA: Harvard Business Review Press, 2018.

Dennett, Daniel. *Consciousness Explained*. Boston, MA: Back Bay Books, 1991.

Dietrich, Arne. *Introduction to Consciousness*. London: Palgrave

Macmillan, 2007.

Easwaran, Eknath, trans. *The Upanishads*. Tomales, CA: Nilgiri Press, 2007.

Flanagan, Owen. *The Bodhisattva's Brain*. Cambridge, MA: A Bradford Book, 2013.

Ford, Martin. *Rise of the Robots*. New York: Basic Books, 2015.

Godman, David. *Be as You Are: The Teaching of Sri Ramana Maharshi*. Delhi, India: Penguin Books, 1992.

Gregory, Jason. *Effortless Living*. Rochester, VT: Inner Traditions, 2018.

Gregory, Jason. *Emotional Intuition for Peak Performance*. Rochester, VT: Inner Traditions, 2020.

Gregory, Jason. *Enlightenment Now*. Rochester, VT: Inner Traditions, 2016.

Gregory, Jason. *Fasting the Mind*. Rochester, VT: Inner Traditions, 2017.

Gregory, Jason. *The Science and Practice of Humility*. Rochester, VT: Inner Traditions, 2014.

Hanh, Thich Nhat. *Silence*. London: Rider, 2015.

Hanson, Rick. *Buddha's Brain*. Oakland, CA: New Harbinger Publications Inc., 2009.

Hart, William. *The Art of Living: Vipassana Meditation*. New York: HarperOne, 1987.

Holiday, Ryan. *Ego is the Enemy*. New York: Portfolio, 2016.

Holiday, Ryan. *The Obstacle is the Way*. New York: Portfolio, 2014.

Husain, Amir. *The Sentient Machine*. New York: Scribner, 2017.

Huxley, Aldous. *The Perennial Philosophy*. New York: Harper Perennial Modern Classics, 2009.

Ivanhoe, Philip J. *The Daodejing of Laozi*. Indianapolis, IN: Hackett Publishing Company, 2003.

Ivanhoe, Philip J., and Bryan W. Van Norden. *Readings in Classical Chinese Philosophy*. Indianapolis, IN: Hackett Publishing Company, 2005.

Kahneman, Daniel. *Thinking, Fast and Slow*. London: Penguin, 2012.

Kaku, Michio. *The Future of Humanity*. New York: Doubleday, 2018.

Kelly, Brendan. *The Yin and Yang of Climate Crisis*. Berkeley, CA: North Atlantic Books, 2015.

Kurzweil, Ray. *The Singularity is Near*. New York: Viking, 2005.

Lanier, Jaron. *Ten Arguments for Deleting Your Social Media Accounts Right Now*. New York: Henry Holt and Company, 2018.

Lao-tzu. *Tao Te Ching: An Illustrated Journey*. Translated by Stephen Mitchell. London: Frances Lincoln, 2009.

Mengzi. *Mengzi*. Translated by Bryan W. Van Norden. Indianapolis, IN: Hackett Publishing, 2008.

Merton, Thomas. *The Way of Chuang Tzu*. New York: New Directions, 2010.

Newport, Cal. *Deep Work*. New York: Grand Central Publishing, 2016.

Newport, Cal. *Digital Minimalism*. London: Penguin, 2019.

Nisbett, Richard E. *The Geography of Thought*. New York: Free Press, 2003.

Olivelle, Patrick. *Upanisads*. New York: Oxford, 1996.

Perlmutter, David. *Brain Maker*. New York: Little, Brown and Company, 2015.

Perlmutter, David. *Grain Brain*. New York: Little, Brown and Company, 2013.

Perlmutter, David. *The Grain Brain Whole Life Plan*. New York: Little, Brown and Company, 2016.

Pinker, Steven. *Enlightenment Now*. New York: Viking, 2018.

Pinker, Steven. *How the Mind Works*. New York: W.W. Norton and Company Inc., 1997.

Pinker, Steven. *The Language Instinct*. New York: Harper Perennial Modern Classics, 2007.

Radhakrishnan, Sarvepalli. *The Bhagavadgita*. Noida, India:

Harper Collins India, 2010.

Ross, Alec. *The Industries of the Future*. New York: Simon & Schuster, 2016.

Selbie, Joseph, and David Steinmetz. *The Yugas*. Nevada City, CA: Crystal Clarity Publishers, 2011.

Shankara. *Shankara's Crest Jewel of Discrimination*. Translated by Swami Prabhavananda and Christopher Isherwood. Los Angeles: Vedanta Society of Southern California, 1975.

Slingerland, Edward, and Mark Collard. *Creating Consilience*. New York: Oxford, 2012.

Slingerland, Edward. *Trying Not to Try*. New York: Broadway Books, 2014.

Suzuki, Daisetz Teitaro, trans. *The Lankavatara Sutra: A Mahayana Text*. Philadelphia, PA: Coronet Books, 1999.

Suzuki, Shunryu. *Zen Mind, Beginner's Mind*. Boston, MA: Shambhala, 2011.

Tegmark, Max. *Life 3.0*. New York: Vintage Books, 2017.

Tsu, Chuang. *Chuang Tsu: Inner Chapters, A Companion Volume to Tao Te Ching*. Translated by Gia-Fu Feng and Jane English. Portland, OR: Amber Lotus, 2008.

Turkle, Sherry. *Reclaiming Conversation*, rev. ed. New York: Penguin, 2016.

Wadhwa, Vivek, and Alex Salkever. *Your Happiness was Hacked*. Oakland, CA: Berrett-Koehler Publishers, Inc., 2018.

Walker, Matthew. *Why We Sleep*. London: Penguin, 2018.

Watts, Alan. *The Book*. New York: Vintage Books, 1989.

Watts, Alan. *The Way of Zen*. New York: Vintage Books, 1999.

Yukteswar, Swami Sri. *The Holy Science*. Los Angeles: Self-Realization Fellowship, 1990.

BOOKS

O-BOOKS

SPIRITUALITY

O is a symbol of the world, of oneness and unity; this eye represents knowledge and insight. We publish titles on general spirituality and living a spiritual life. We aim to inform and help you on your own journey in this life.

If you have enjoyed this book, why not tell other readers by posting a review on your preferred book site?

Recent bestsellers from O-Books are:

Heart of Tantric Sex
Diana Richardson
Revealing Eastern secrets of deep love and intimacy to Western couples.
Paperback: 978-1-90381-637-0 ebook: 978-1-84694-637-0

Crystal Prescriptions
The A-Z guide to over 1,200 symptoms and their healing crystals
Judy Hall
The first in the popular series of eight books, this handy little guide is packed as tight as a pill-bottle with crystal remedies for ailments.
Paperback: 978-1-90504-740-6 ebook: 978-1-84694-629-5

Take Me To Truth
Undoing the Ego
Nouk Sanchez, Tomas Vieira
The best-selling step-by-step book on shedding the Ego, using the teachings of *A Course In Miracles*.
Paperback: 978-1-84694-050-7 ebook: 978-1-84694-654-7

The 7 Myths about Love...Actually!
The Journey from your HEAD to the HEART of your SOUL
Mike George
Smashes all the myths about LOVE.
Paperback: 978-1-84694-288-4 ebook: 978-1-84694-682-0

The Holy Spirit's Interpretation of the New Testament
A Course in Understanding and Acceptance
Regina Dawn Akers
Following on from the strength of *A Course In Miracles*, NTI
teaches us how to experience the love and oneness of God.
Paperback: 978-1-84694-085-9 ebook: 978-1-78099-083-5

The Message of A Course In Miracles
A translation of the Text in plain language
Elizabeth A. Cronkhite
A translation of *A Course in Miracles* into plain, everyday
language for anyone seeking inner peace. The companion
volume, *Practicing A Course In Miracles*, offers practical lessons
and mentoring.
Paperback: 978-1-84694-319-5 ebook: 978-1-84694-642-4

Your Simple Path
Find Happiness in every step
Ian Tucker
A guide to helping us reconnect with what is really important in
our lives.
Paperback: 978-1-78279-349-6 ebook: 978-1-78279-348-9

365 Days of Wisdom
Daily Messages To Inspire You Through The Year
Dadi Janki
Daily messages which cool the mind, warm the heart and guide
you along your journey.
Paperback: 978-1-84694-863-3 ebook: 978-1-84694-864-0

Body of Wisdom
Women's Spiritual Power and How it Serves
Hilary Hart
Bringing together the dreams and experiences of women across
the world with today's most visionary spiritual teachers.
Paperback: 978-1-78099-696-7 ebook: 978-1-78099-695-0

Dying to Be Free
From Enforced Secrecy to Near Death to True Transformation
Hannah Robinson
After an unexpected accident and near-death experience, Hannah
Robinson found herself radically transforming her life, while a
remarkable new insight altered her relationship with her father, a
practising Catholic priest.
Paperback: 978-1-78535-254-6 ebook: 978-1-78535-255-3

The Ecology of the Soul
A Manual of Peace, Power and Personal Growth for Real People
in the Real World
Aidan Walker
Balance your own inner Ecology of the Soul to regain your
natural state of peace, power and wellbeing.
Paperback: 978-1-78279-850-7 ebook: 978-1-78279-849-1

Not I, Not other than I
The Life and Teachings of Russel Williams
Steve Taylor, Russel Williams
The miraculous life and inspiring teachings of one of the World's
greatest living Sages.
Paperback: 978-1-78279-729-6 ebook: 978-1-78279-728-9

On the Other Side of Love
A woman's unconventional journey towards wisdom
Muriel Maufroy
When life has lost all meaning, what do you do?
Paperback: 978-1-78535-281-2 ebook: 978-1-78535-282-9

Practicing A Course In Miracles
A translation of the Workbook in plain language, with
mentor's notes
Elizabeth A. Cronkhite
The practical second and third volumes of The Plain-Language
A Course In Miracles.
Paperback: 978-1-84694-403-1 ebook: 978-1-78099-072-9

Quantum Bliss
The Quantum Mechanics of Happiness, Abundance, and Health
George S. Mentz
Quantum Bliss is the breakthrough summary of success and
spirituality secrets that customers have been waiting for.
Paperback: 978-1-78535-203-4 ebook: 978-1-78535-204-1

The Upside Down Mountain
Mags MacKean
A must-read for anyone weary of chasing success and happiness
– one woman's inspirational journey swapping the uphill slog for
the downhill slope.
Paperback: 978-1-78535-171-6 ebook: 978-1-78535-172-3

Your Personal Tuning Fork
The Endocrine System
Deborah Bates
Discover your body's health secret, the endocrine system, and
'twang' your way to sustainable health!
Paperback: 978-1-84694-503-8 ebook: 978-1-78099-697-4

Readers of ebooks can buy or view any of these bestsellers by clicking on the live link in the title. Most titles are published in paperback and as an ebook. Paperbacks are available in traditional bookshops. Both print and ebook formats are available online.
Find more titles and sign up to our readers' newsletter at
http://www.johnhuntpublishing.com/mind-body-spirit
Follow us on Facebook at https://www.facebook.com/OBooks/
and Twitter at https://twitter.com/obooks